Southern Bean

240 Recipes for Soups, Casseroles, Meals, Salads & Side Dishes!

S. L. Watson

Copyright © 2015 S. L. Watson

All rights reserved.

ISBN:9781549632310

No part of this book may be reproduced or utilized in any form or by any means, electronic or mechanical, including photocopying and recording without express written permission from the author and/or copyright holder. This book is for informational or entertainment purposes only.

Cover design S. L. Watson 2015. Picture courtesy of Canva. The author has made every effort to ensure the information provided in this book is correct. Failure to follow directions could result in a failed recipe. The author does not assume and hereby disclaim any liability to any party for any loss, damage, illness or disruption caused by errors and omissions, whether such errors and omissions result from negligence, accident or any other cause.

The author has made every effort to provide accurate information in the creation of this book. The author accepts no responsibility and gives no warranty for any damages or loss of any kind that might be incurred by the reader or user due to actions resulting from the use of the information in this book. The user assumes complete responsibility for the use of the information in this book.

DEDICATION

To my family for being valiant and honest taste testers!

CONTENTS

	Introduction & How To Cook Dried Beans	i
1	Bean Soups & Stews	1
2	Pinto Beans	41
3	Kidney Beans	63
4	Lentils	82
5	Black Beans	96
6	Great Northern & Navy Beans	118
7	Garbanzo Beans	136
8	Salads	144
9	Black Eye Peas	173
10	Lima Beans	199

Introduction

Beans are a budget friendly and healthy way to eat whole foods. Whether you prefer to cook dry beans or use frozen or canned beans, you will find 240 recipes to feed your family. Included are recipes for soups, casseroles, main dishes and side dishes.

I've included recipes for lentils, pinto beans, black beans, great northern beans, kidney beans, black eye peas and lima beans. Also included are numerous salad recipes. Beans make a wonderful warm or chilled salad. They are a great alternative to meat proteins in salads and main dishes.

Cooked beans are easy to freeze and great for quick and easy meals. I cook beans all the time in the crock pot. We eat them for dinner and I freeze the remainder of the beans. When I want to make a recipe that calls for cooked beans, cooked beans are already in the freezer.

Most of the soup recipes and many main dish recipes can be made ahead and frozen for future meals. Freezer meals make it so easy when you need a meal in a hurry.

How to Cook Dried Beans

There are two methods I use for soaking dried beans. The cooking time is reduced and I think dried beans taste better when soaked. Always wash dried beans before using. Sort through the beans to double check for bad beans or small stones. Discard any bad beans or stones.

Once dried beans come to a boil, reduce the heat. If dried beans are cooked too fast, the skins will break. A simmer is best for cooking beans. Simmering the beans produces a rich and delicious broth. I do not add salt in most recipes until the last 20 minutes of cooking time.

Quick Soaking Method

Add the beans to a large pot. Add cold water to about 2" above the beans. Bring the beans to a boil over medium to medium high heat. Boil for 2-4 minutes. Remove the beans from the heat and place a lid on the pot. Let the beans soak for 1-2 hours.

Overnight Method

This is my preferred method for soaking beans. I let my beans soak for 24-36 hours. You will see bubbles on the beans when soaking for an extended time. This eliminates a lot of gas from the beans.

Place the beans in a large pot. Cover the beans with cold water about 3" above the beans. Let the beans soak at least 8 hours but no longer than 36 hours. Drain the beans after soaking and rinse with cold water. Add fresh water to cook the beans.

You can easily freeze dried cooked beans. I almost always cook my beans in a crock pot. You can cook the beans on low or high temperature. Cool the beans overnight and then spoon the beans into freezer bags. I freeze my beans in 2 cup increments. Lay the beans in the refrigerator overnight to thaw. Depending upon the recipe, you may be able to add the frozen beans directly to the recipe.

Always season beans to your taste with salt and black pepper. I add minced garlic and onions to black beans while cooking. It really gives the beans a wonderful flavor and the flavor will not be prominent in your recipe. The garlic and onion enhance the flavor of the black beans.

1 BEAN SOUPS & STEWS

Soups and stews are an economical way to use beans. You can feed your family inexpensively and healthy with soups and stews.

I have included my family favorite soups. In the wintertime, we love a wide variety of soups. Bean soups really stick to your ribs on a cold winter night. I serve the soups with hot cornbread or biscuits.

White Bean Chowder with Sage Pesto

Makes 8 cups

1 1/2 cups dried great northern beans
Water
2 bacon slices
1 onion, minced
3 garlic cloves, minced
2 carrots, chopped
2 celery stalks, chopped
3 1/2 cups chicken broth
1 bay leaf
2 cups diced red potatoes
29 oz. can diced tomatoes
1/2 tsp. salt
1/2 tsp. black pepper
1/4 cup fresh sage leaves
2/3 cup Italian parsley
2 tbs. pine nuts
2 garlic cloves, peeled
2 tbs. freshly grated Parmesan cheese
2 tbs. olive oil

Rinse the beans with cold water and remove any bad beans. Place the beans in a dutch oven. Cover the beans with cold water about 3" above the beans. Place a lid on the pot and soak the beans for 8-12 hours. After soaking, drain all the water from the beans. Rinse the beans with cold water and drain again. In a skillet over medium heat, add the bacon. Cook the bacon about 5 minutes or until the bacon is crisp. Remove the bacon from the skillet and drain on paper towels. Crumble the bacon into pieces.

Add the onion and 3 minced garlic cloves to the bacon drippings in the skillet. Saute the onion and garlic about 4 minutes. Remove the skillet from the heat and add the onion, garlic and any drippings to the beans. Add the carrots, celery, chicken broth and bay leaf to the beans. Place the beans over medium heat. When the beans are boiling, place a lid on the pot. Reduce the heat to low and simmer about 1 1/2 hours or until the beans are almost tender. Stir the beans occasionally to keep the ingredients from sticking. Add the potatoes and simmer about 20 minutes or until the potatoes and beans are tender. Stir in the tomatoes, salt and black pepper. Remove the chowder from the heat.

To make the pesto, add the sage leaves, parsley, pine nuts, 2 peeled garlic cloves, Parmesan cheese and olive oil to a food processor. Process until smooth. Place the chowder in soup bowls. Spoon the pesto over the top of the soup and serve.

Spicy Chicken Bean Chili

Makes 6 servings

1 1/2 lbs. boneless chicken thighs, cut into bite size pieces
1 tsp. salt
1 tsp. black pepper
2 tbs. vegetable oil
3 1/2 cups chopped onion
1 tbs. minced fresh garlic
1/3 cup tomato paste
1 1/2 tbs. chili powder
1 1/2 tsp. ground cumin
8 cups chicken broth
4 cups cooked kidney beans
2 cans fire roasted tomatoes, 14 oz. size
16 oz. bag frozen black eye peas, thawed
2 cups cooked pinto beans

Season the chicken with salt and black pepper. In a large pot over medium heat, add the vegetable oil. When the oil is hot, add the chicken. Stir frequently and cook about 5 minutes or until the chicken is golden brown. Remove the chicken from the pot and set aside.

Add the onion and garlic to the pan. Saute for 10 minutes or until the onion is tender. Stir in the tomato paste, chili powder and ground cumin. Stir constantly and cook for 1 minute. Add the chicken broth, kidney beans, tomatoes, black eye peas, pinto beans and chicken. Stir constantly until the chili is boiling. When the chili is boiling, reduce the heat to low. Stir frequently and simmer the chili for 1 hour. Remove the pan from the heat and serve.

Vegetarian Chili

Makes about 3 quarts

1 lb. dried kidney beans
Water
1 cup tomato juice
1 cup bulgur wheat
2 garlic cloves, crushed
1 1/2 cups chopped onion
2 cups chopped fresh or canned tomatoes
1 cup chopped carrot
1 cup chopped celery
1 cup chopped green bell pepper
6 oz. can tomato paste
1/2 cup dry red wine
2 tbs. lemon juice
1 1/2 tsp. ground cumin
1 1/2 tsp. chili powder
1 tsp. dried basil
1/2 tsp. salt
1/4 tsp. black pepper

Sort and wash the kidney beans in cold water. Add the beans and 3 cups water to a large pot. Place the beans on the stove over medium heat and bring the beans to a boil. Boil the beans for 3 minutes and remove the beans from the heat. Place a lid on the pot and let the beans soak for 1 1/2 hours.

Add 4 cups water to the pot. Place the pot back on the stove over medium heat and bring the beans to a boil. When the beans are boiling, reduce the heat to low. Place a lid on the pot and simmer for 1 to 1 1/2 hours or until the beans are tender. Remove the beans from the heat and set aside for now. In a mixing bowl, add the bulgur wheat. Heat the tomato juice in a pan or in the microwave until the tomato juice boils. Pour the tomato juice over the bulgur. Stir the bulgur and set aside for now.

Spray a large sauce pan with non stick cooking spray. Add the garlic and onion to the sauce pan. Place the pan over medium heat and saute the onion and garlic for 4 minutes. Add the tomatoes, 2 cups water, carrot, celery, green bell pepper, tomato paste, red wine, lemon juice, cumin, chili powder, basil, salt and black pepper. Stir until well combined. Bring the vegetables to a boil. Reduce the heat to low and place a lid on the pan. Simmer the vegetables for 20 minutes. Remove the pan from the heat and add the vegetables to the beans. Add the bulgur to the beans and stir until combined. Place the bean pot back on the stove over medium heat. Heat only until the chili begins to bubble. Remove the pot from the heat and serve.

Vegetarian Pinto Bean Chili

Makes 6 servings

1 cup dried pinto beans
Water
16 oz. can whole kernel corn, undrained
15 oz. can tomato sauce
1 large onion, chopped
4 oz. can diced green chiles, drained
1 garlic clove, minced
1 tsp. salt
2 tsp. chili powder
1 tsp. dried oregano
1 bay leaf

In a large pot, add the beans. Cover the beans with cold water about 3" above the beans. Place a lid on the pot and let the beans soak for 24 hours. Pour the water off the beans and rinse the beans with fresh cold water. Drain all the water from the beans.

Add 4 cups water to the beans and place the beans on the stove over medium heat. Bring the beans to a rolling boil and reduce the heat to medium low. Stir in the corn, tomato sauce, onion, green chiles, garlic, salt, chili powder, oregano and bay leaf. Stir until well combined.

Simmer the chili for 2 1/2 hours or until the beans are tender. Remove the bay leaf from the pot and discard. Remove the pot from the heat and serve.

Cow Puncher's Bean Stew

Makes 6 servings

1 lb. dry pinto beans
Water
1/2 tsp. ground cumin
2 garlic cloves, minced
2 tbs. salt
2 tbs. bacon fat
1 small red chili pepper, finely diced, optional

You can soak the beans overnight or cook them straight from the bag. Use whichever method you prefer.

In a large stock pot over medium heat, add the pinto beans, cumin and garlic. Add cold water to about 2" above the beans. When the beans are boiling, place a lid on the pan and reduce the heat to low. The beans need to stay at a simmer. Simmer the beans for 1 1/2 hours.

You may need to add more water to the beans. The beans need to stay covered with water. If you did not soak the beans, they will absorb extra water. Add the salt and bacon fat. Stir occasionally and cook until the beans are tender. This may take an hour or two depending upon whether you soaked the beans or not. Remove the pot from the heat and sprinkle the red chili pepper over the top.

Serve in bowls with hot cornbread or serve over rice. I serve this with smoked sausage slices over the top of each serving.

Guadalajara Soup

Makes about 8 cups

1 1/4 cups dried pinto beans
Water
1/4 cup vegetable oil
3 1/2 lbs. country style pork ribs
1 cup finely chopped onion
2 garlic cloves, minced
3 1/2 cups beef broth
2 tsp. chili powder
1 tsp. dried oregano
1 tsp. ground cumin
1/2 tsp. salt
1/4 tsp. black pepper
4 cups thinly sliced carrots
7 oz. jar baby corn on the cob
Sour cream, optional
Salsa, optional

Rinse the beans with cold water and remove any bad beans. Place the beans in a dutch oven. Cover the beans with cold water about 2" above the beans. Place the beans on the stove over medium heat. Bring the beans to a boil and cook for 2 minutes. Remove the pan from the heat and place a lid on the pan. Soak the beans for 1 hour. When the beans have soaked for 1 hour, drain all the water from the beans.

In a large skillet over medium heat, add the vegetable oil. When the oil is hot, add the ribs. Brown the ribs about 5 minutes on each side or until the ribs are well browned. Remove the ribs from the skillet and set aside but leave any drippings in the skillet. Add the onion and garlic to the skillet. Saute the onion and garlic for 3 minutes. Remove the skillet from the heat. Add the onion and garlic with any pan drippings to the beans. Add the ribs, beef broth, 4 cups water, chili powder, oregano, cumin, salt and black pepper to the beans. Place the pan on the stove over medium high heat. When the beans are boiling, place a lid on the pan and reduce the heat to low. Simmer for 1 1/2 to 2 hours or until the beans are tender and the ribs done. Remove the pan from the heat. Remove the ribs from the pan. Remove all the meat from the bones and add the meat back to the pan. Discard the bones. Let the beans chill until the grease rises to the top of the soup. Skim off the grease and discard.

Place the beans on the stove over medium heat. When the beans are boiling, add the carrots and corn. Simmer for 30 minutes or until the carrots are tender. Add water as needed to keep the beans and meat covered in liquid. You can use additional beef broth instead of water for additional flavor. Remove the soup from the heat and serve with sour cream and salsa if desired.

Simple Mexican Puchero

Makes 6 servings

1/4 lb. salt pork, diced
3 cups cubed boneless beef (I use round steak)
1 garlic clove, minced
1 cup chopped cabbage
1 tsp. dried oregano, crumbled
1/2 tsp. ground coriander
1/2 tsp. ground cumin
2 1/2 cups canned diced tomatoes
2 tbs. fresh minced parsley
3/4 cup soaked dried garbanzo beans
1/3 cup uncooked rice
Water
1 cup whole kernel corn, fresh, frozen or canned
Salt and black pepper to taste

In a large skillet over medium heat, add the salt pork. Stir frequently and cook until the salt pork is crispy on all sides. The pork will have released some of the fat. Add the beef, garlic, cabbage, oregano, coriander, cumin, tomatoes with liquid, parsley, garbanzo beans and rice to the skillet. Add water to cover the beans, meat and vegetables in the skillet.

Bring the meat and vegetables to a boil. When the liquid is boiling, place a lid on the skillet and reduce the heat to low. Stir occasionally and simmer for 1 1/2 hours. The beef should be done and the garbanzo beans tender when ready. Remove the lid from the skillet.

Stir in the corn and season to taste with salt and black pepper. Cook until the corn is tender. Remove the skillet from the heat and serve. Season with additional cumin if desired.

Spicy Three Bean Soup

Makes about 2 1/2 quarts

2 bone in skinless chicken breast, about 8 oz. each
3 cups water
28 oz. can diced tomatoes
10 oz. pkg. frozen cut green beans
10 oz. pkg. frozen lima beans
1 bay leaf
2 tsp. Creole seasoning
1 tsp. chili powder
1 tsp. paprika
1/4 tsp. garlic powder
1/4 tsp. onion powder
1/4 tsp. cayenne pepper
1/8 tsp. Tabasco sauce
1/8 tsp. soy sauce
1/8 tsp. Worcestershire sauce
15 oz. can black beans, drained

In a dutch oven, add the chicken breast, water, tomatoes with juice, green beans, lima beans, bay leaf, Creole seasoning, chili powder, paprika, garlic powder, onion powder, cayenne pepper, Tabasco sauce, soy sauce and Worcestershire sauce. Stir until well combined.

Place the pan over medium heat and bring to a boil. When the soup is boiling, reduce the heat to low and simmer for 1 hour. Remove the bay leaf and chicken breast. Remove the meat from the chicken and discard the bay leaf. Add the chicken meat back to the soup along with the black beans. Simmer for 5 minutes. Remove the pan from the heat and serve.

Mexican Black Bean Soup

Makes about 11 cups

1 lb. dried black beans
Water
6 cups chicken broth
2 small ham hocks
1/4 lb. salt pork
1 bay leaf
1 cup chopped onion
1/2 cup chopped celery with leaves
1 1/2 cups chopped green bell pepper
1 large tomato, peeled and chopped
1 garlic clove, minced
6 serrano peppers, seeded and chopped
6 oz. can tomato paste
1/4 tsp. black pepper
1/4 tsp. Tabasco sauce
2 tbs. Worcestershire sauce
Lemon slices, optional

Rinse the beans with cold water and remove any bad beans. Add the beans to a large pot. Cover the beans with cold water about 3" above the beans. Place a lid on the pot and soak the beans for 12 hours. When the beans have soaked, drain all the water from the beans. Rinse the beans with cold water and drain again.

Add the chicken broth, 2 cups water, ham hocks, salt pork and bay leaf to the beans in the pot. Place the pot on the stove over medium heat and bring the beans to a boil. When the beans are boiling, place a lid on the pot. Reduce the heat to low and simmer the beans for 1 1/2 hours. The beans will not be done at this point.

Remove the ham hocks and salt pork from the beans. Remove any meat from the hocks and discard the bones and salt pork. Add the meat back to the pot of beans. Stir in the onion, celery, green bell pepper, tomato, garlic, serrano peppers, tomato paste, black pepper, Tabasco sauce and Worcestershire sauce. Bring the beans to a boil and place the lid back on the pot. Simmer the beans for 1 1/2 hours or until the beans are tender.

Mash the beans in the pot with a potato masher. You do not want all the beans mashed but the beans should still be chunky. Remove the pot from the heat. Spoon the soup into bowls and squeeze the lemon slices over the top.

One Skillet Chili Bake

Makes 6 servings

1 lb. ground beef
15 oz. can red kidney beans, drained
10 oz. can Rotel tomatoes
1 cup water
1/2 cup uncooked long grain rice
2 tbs. chili powder
1 cup shredded cheddar cheese
Diced tomatoes, green onions and tortilla chips, optional

In a large skillet over medium heat, add the ground beef. Stir frequently and break the meat into crumbles as it cooks. Cook for 7-8 minutes or until the ground beef is well browned and no longer pink. Drain off the excess grease.

Stir in the kidney beans, Rotel tomatoes with liquid, water, rice and chili powder. Bring the mixture to a boil. Place a lid on the skillet and reduce the heat to low. Simmer for 20 minutes or until the rice is tender.

Remove the lid from the skillet. Sprinkle the cheddar cheese over the top of the dish. Sprinkle with diced tomatoes and green onions if desired. Serve with tortilla chips if desired.

Bean and Pasta Soup

Makes 12 servings

1 1/2 lbs. lean ground beef
5 cups beef broth
1 1/2 cups V-8 juice
28 oz. can crushed tomatoes
6 oz. can tomato paste
1 1/2 cups chopped onion
1 1/2 cups chopped celery with leaves
1 1/2 cups shredded carrot
15 oz. can kidney beans, rinsed and drained
15 oz. can great northern beans, rinsed and drained
1/4 cup lemon juice
2 tsp. dried Italian seasoning
2 tsp. cayenne pepper
1/2 tsp. salt
3 cups cooked small pasta

In a large dutch oven over medium heat, add the ground beef. Stir frequently to break the meat into crumbles as it cooks. Cook about 6 minutes or until the ground beef is well browned and no longer pink. Drain off any excess grease.

Stir in the beef broth, V-8 juice, crushed tomatoes with juice, tomato paste, onion, celery, carrot, kidney beans, great northern beans, lemon juice, Italian seasoning, cayenne pepper and salt. Bring the soup to a boil and reduce the heat to low. Simmer the soup for 30 minutes. Stir in the pasta and simmer for 5 minutes. Remove the soup from the heat and serve.

You can freeze the soup if desired. Omit the pasta if freezing the soup. Add the cooked pasta to the soup when reheating.

Carolina Black Bean Soup

Makes 10 servings

1 lb. dried black beans
8 cups water
1 cup chopped onion
1 cup chopped celery
1 cup chopped green bell pepper
1 garlic clove, minced
1 tbs. olive oil
1 tsp. salt
1 tsp. black pepper
3 cups tomato sauce

Rinse the beans with cold water and remove any bad beans. Add the beans to a large dutch oven or stock pot. Add the water and bring the beans to a boil over medium high heat. Boil the beans for 3 minutes. Remove the beans from the heat and place a lid on the pan. Let the beans soak for 1 hour.

In a skillet over medium heat, add the onion, celery, green bell pepper, garlic and olive oil. Saute the vegetables for 5 minutes. When the beans have soaked, add the vegetables to the beans. Add the salt and black pepper to the beans. Stir until combined.

Place the beans back on the stove over medium high heat and cook until the beans are boiling. Reduce the heat to low and place a lid on the pot. Simmer the beans for 1 1/2 to 2 hours or until the beans are tender. Stir in the tomato sauce and simmer the beans for 30 minutes. Remove the soup from the heat and serve.

Spanish Chick Pea Soup

Makes 8 servings

1 3/4 cups dried chick peas
4 cups cold water
1 minced garlic clove
2 onions, chopped
1 green bell pepper, chopped
1 tbs. vegetable oil
4 cups ham broth
1 large potato, diced
1/3 cup diced cooked ham
1/2 lb. cooked chorizo sausage, sliced
Salt and cayenne pepper to taste

In a dutch oven, add the chick peas and water. Place a lid on the pot and soak the chick peas at least 12 hours. Do not drain the water from the chick peas once they have soaked.

In a skillet over medium heat, add the garlic, onions, green bell pepper and vegetable oil. Saute the vegetables for 5 minutes. Remove the skillet from the heat and add the vegetables to the chick peas.

Place the chick peas on the stove over medium high heat. Add the ham broth and bring the peas to a boil. When the peas are boiling, reduce the heat to medium. Simmer the chick peas about 2 hours or until the chick peas are tender.

Add the potato, ham and chorizo to the pot. Simmer for 30 minutes. Season to taste with salt and cayenne pepper. Remove the soup from the heat and serve.

Western Bean Stew

Makes 6 servings

1 lb. dried pinto beans
Water
Ham bone
1 tsp. salt
1/8 tsp. Tabasco sauce
1/4 cup bacon grease
1 large onion, chopped
1 garlic clove, minced
4 medium fresh tomatoes, chopped or 1 1/2 cups diced canned tomatoes
1/4 cup fresh minced parsley
1/2 tsp. ground marjoram
1 tbs. chili powder

Soak the dried pinto beans overnight. To soak the beans, place the beans in a large pot. Cover the beans with cold water about 3" above the beans. Let the beans soak at least 8 hours but no longer than 36 hours. Drain the beans after soaking and rinse with cold water.

Add the beans to a dutch oven or stock pot. Add the ham bone, salt and Tabasco sauce. Cover the beans with cold water and bring the beans to a boil over medium heat. When the beans are at a full boil, reduce the heat to medium low. Place a lid on the pot and simmer the beans for 1 1/2 hours or until the beans are tender. Remove the beans from the heat. Drain the beans but reserve the cooking liquid.

Add the bacon grease to a large skillet over medium heat. When the bacon grease melts, add the onion and garlic. Stir frequently and cook until the onion is golden brown. Add the tomatoes, parsley, marjoram, chili powder and 1 cup reserved bean liquid. Stir frequently and bring the mixture to a boil. Reduce the heat to low. Season with additional salt and chili powder if desired. Place a lid on the skillet and simmer for 40 minutes. Add the beans to the skillet and simmer for 15 minutes. Remove the skillet from the heat and remove the ham bone, Discard the ham bone.

Baked Bean Winter Soup

Makes 6 servings

2 cans pork & beans, 15 oz. size
16 oz. can diced tomatoes
1 onion, chopped
2 celery stalks, sliced
1 tsp. Worcestershire sauce
4 cups water
1/4 tsp. Tabasco sauce
1 lb. cooked smoked sausage, sliced

In a large sauce pan over medium heat, add the pork & beans, tomatoes with juice, onion, celery, Worcestershire sauce, water and Tabasco sauce. Stir frequently and bring the soup to a boil. When the soup is boiling, reduce the heat to low. Simmer the soup 15 minutes. Stir in the smoked sausage and simmer for 15 minutes. Remove the soup from the heat and serve. Delicious served with hot cornbread or hearty rolls.

Cabbage Bean Soup

Makes 6 servings

1 tbs. vegetable oil
1 onion, diced
2 cups water
29 oz. can Mexican style diced tomatoes
8 oz. diced cooked ham
10 oz. pkg. shredded fresh cabbage
2 tsp. chili seasoning mix
1/4 tsp. black pepper
16 oz. can great northern beans, rinsed and drained

In a dutch oven over medium heat, add the onion and vegetable oil. Saute the onion about 5 minutes or until the onion is tender. Drain off the excess grease from the pan.

Add the water, tomatoes with juice, ham, cabbage, chili seasoning mix and black pepper. Stir until well combined and bring the soup to a boil. When the soup is boiling, reduce the heat to low. Simmer the soup for 15 minutes. Add the great northern beans and simmer the soup for 15 minutes. Remove the pan from the heat and serve.

Senate Bean Soup

Makes about 1 gallon. This soup freezes well.

1 lb. dried white beans
Water
1 smoked ham hock
3 potatoes, cooked and mashed
2 onions, chopped
1 cup celery, diced
2 garlic cloves, minced
Salt and black pepper to taste

In a large pot, add the dried white beans. Cover the beans with water and place the beans on the stove over medium heat. Bring the beans to a boil and cook for 2 minutes. Remove the beans from the heat and place a lid on the pot. Let the beans soak for 1 hour.

Drain the beans but save the liquid. Measure the bean liquid and add water to make 5 quarts liquid. Add the liquids to the beans in the pot. Bring the beans to a boil over medium heat and reduce the heat to medium low. Simmer the beans for 2 hours or until the beans are tender. Add the ham hock, potatoes, onions, celery and garlic cloves. Stir frequently and cook for 1 hour.

Remove the ham hock from the beans. Remove the meat from the ham hock and chop into pieces. Add the meat back to the pot. Stir until well combined and season to taste with salt and black pepper. Remove the soup from the heat and serve.

Sausage, Spinach and Bean Soup

Makes 8 servings

8 oz. ground Italian sausage
1 tsp. olive oil
5 garlic cloves, minced
1/2 tsp. dried crushed red pepper flakes
2 bags torn fresh spinach, 10 oz. size
2 cans cannellini beans, 15 oz. size
3 cups chicken broth
1/4 cup unsalted butter
1/2 cup freshly shredded Parmesan cheese
2 plum tomatoes, diced
2 tbs. chopped fresh parsley
1/4 tsp. salt
1/4 tsp. black pepper

In a large dutch oven over medium heat, add the Italian sausage and olive oil. Stir the sausage frequently to break the meat into crumbles as it cooks. Cook about 8 minutes or until the sausage is well browned and no longer pink. Add the garlic and red pepper flakes to the pan. Stir frequently and cook for 2 minutes. Add the spinach and stir until the spinach begins to wilt.

Stir in the cannellini beans and cook for 1 minute. Stir in the chicken broth and bring the soup to a boil. When the soup is boiling, add the butter, Parmesan cheese, tomatoes, parsley, salt and black pepper. Stir constantly and cook for 2 minutes. Remove the pot from the heat and serve.

Refried Bean Soup

Makes 7 cups

6 corn tortillas
1 onion, chopped
2 garlic cloves, minced
1 tbs. vegetable oil
31 oz. can refried beans
16 oz. can diced tomatoes
10 oz. can diced tomatoes with green chiles
1 3/4 cups chicken broth
2 tbs. chopped fresh cilantro
2 cups shredded Monterey Jack cheese
1 cup sour cream

Preheat the oven to 350°. Cut the corn tortillas into thin strips. Place the strips on a baking sheet. Bake the tortilla strips for 15 minutes. Stir the tortilla strips every 5 minutes. Remove the tortillas from the oven.

In a large sauce pan or dutch oven over medium heat, add the onion, garlic and vegetable oil. Saute the onion and garlic for 4 minutes. Add the refried beans, tomatoes with liquid, tomatoes with green chiles and liquid, chicken broth and cilantro to the pan. Stir frequently until the soup is boiling. Cook for 15 minutes. Remove the soup from the heat.

Spoon the soup into bowls. Sprinkle the corn tortillas over the top. Sprinkle the Monterey Jack cheese over the tortillas. Spoon sour cream over the cheese and serve.

Tuscany Bean Soup

Makes 8 servings

1 lb. dried great northern beans
Water
1 1/4 cups chicken broth
1/2 tsp. dried marjoram leaves
1 bay leaf
1/8 tsp. black pepper
2 tbs. vegetable oil
1 1/2 cups sliced onion
1 minced garlic clove
1 cup carrots, sliced
2 potatoes, julienned
1 tbs. salt
10 oz. pkg. frozen spinach, thawed
1/2 cup grated Parmesan cheese

Place the beans in a large pot. Cover the beans with cold water to about 3" above the beans. Soak the beans overnight or about 12 hours. Drain the soaking water from the beans. Rinse the beans well with cold water.

Add 12 cups cold water to the beans. Bring the beans to a boil over medium heat. Add the chicken broth, marjoram, bay leaf and black pepper. Stir until combined and simmer the beans for 1 hour.

In a skillet over medium heat, add the vegetable oil. When the oil is hot, add the onion, garlic and carrots. Saute the vegetables for 5-6 minutes or until the onions are browned. Remove the skillet from the heat and add the vegetables to the beans. Add the potatoes, salt and spinach to the beans. Place a lid on the pot and simmer for 1 1/2 to 2 hours or until the beans are tender. Remove the soup from the heat and ladle into bowls. Sprinkle the Parmesan cheese over each serving.

White Bean Soup

Makes 10-12 servings

2 lbs. dried great northern beans
Water
2 cups diced cooked ham
1 cup diced celery
1 cup sliced carrots
1/2 cup chopped green onions
1 minced red chile pepper, optional
16 oz. can diced tomatoes
1 1/2 tsp. salt
1/2 tsp. black pepper

Place the beans in a large pot. Cover the beans with cold water to about 3" above the beans. Let the beans soak at least 8 hours but no longer than 36 hours. Drain the beans after soaking and rinse with cold water.

In a large pot, add the soaked beans and 4 quarts water. Bring the beans to a boil over medium high heat. Once the beans are boiling, reduce the heat to medium. Place a lid on the beans and simmer for 1 1/2 hours. Stir occasionally to keep the beans from sticking. Add water if needed to keep the beans covered in water.

Stir in the ham, celery, carrots, green onions and chile pepper. Simmer for 45 minutes. The beans should be tender. Stir in the tomatoes with juice, salt and black pepper. Simmer for 15 minutes. Remove the soup from the heat and serve.

Portuguese Bean Soup

Makes 3 quarts

1 cup dried red beans
2 quarts water
1/4 cup bacon grease
3 onions, sliced
2 garlic cloves, minced
6 potatoes, diced
2 bay leaves
1 tsp. ground allspice
8 oz. can tomato paste
Salt and black pepper to taste

In a large pot, add the beans and water. Place the pot over medium heat and bring the beans to a boil. Boil for 2 minutes. Remove the beans from the heat and place a lid on the pot. Let the beans soak for 1 hour.

Place the beans back on the stove over medium heat and bring the beans to a full boil. When the beans are boiling, reduce the heat to medium low. Simmer the beans for 1 1/2 hours.

In a skillet over medium heat, add the bacon grease, onions and garlic. Saute the onions and garlic for 3-4 minutes. The onions should be lightly browned. Remove the skillet from the heat and add the vegetables including the bacon grease to the beans. Add the potatoes, bay leaves, allspice and tomato paste to the beans.

Stir until well combined. Place the lid back on the pot and simmer for 1 to 1 1/2 hours or until the beans and potatoes are tender. Remove the beans from the heat. Season to taste with salt and black pepper. Remove the bay leaves and serve.

Kidney Bean Soup with Walnuts

Makes 6 servings

1 lb. dried red kidney beans
Water
7 cups chicken broth
1/2 tsp. salt
2 large onions, finely chopped
3 garlic cloves, minced
1/4 cup olive oil
1/2 cup finely chopped walnuts
3 tbs. tarragon vinegar
2 tsp. crushed coriander seeds
1/2 tsp. black pepper
1/2 cup chopped fresh cilantro
1/4 cup chopped fresh parsley

Add the kidney beans to a large pot. Add cold water to about 3" above the beans. Place a lid on the pot and soak the beans for 12 hours. Drain all the water from the beans. Rinse the beans with cold water and drain the beans again. Add the chicken broth to the beans. Place the pot over medium high heat until the beans come to a boil. When the beans are boiling, reduce the heat to medium low. Place a lid on the pot and simmer the beans about 1 1/2 to 2 hours or until they are tender.

Drain the beans but reserve 3 cups bean liquid. If you do not have 3 cups liquid, add additional chicken broth or water to the reserved liquid. Using the back of a spoon, mash the kidney beans. You do not want the beans totally mashed. The beans still need to have chunky pieces. Add the bean liquid back to the beans in the pot along with the salt. Simmer the beans for 5 minutes and remove the beans from the heat.

In a skillet over medium heat, add the onions, garlic and olive oil. Saute the onions and garlic about 5 minutes. Add the walnuts, tarragon vinegar, coriander seeds and black pepper. Stir until well combined. Remove the skillet from the heat and stir the walnut mixture into the beans. Spoon the soup into bowls and sprinkle the parsley and cilantro over each serving.

Bean and Hominy Soup

Makes 12 cups

I love this soup using pantry ingredients. It is quick to make and provides a hearty meal in less than an hour.

3 cans great northern beans, 15 oz. size
15 oz. can hominy
14 oz. can stewed tomatoes
11 oz. can condensed bean with bacon soup
10 oz. can diced tomatoes and green chiles
15 oz. can whole kernel corn
2 cups water
2 bay leaves
1 tbs. dried cilantro
1 tsp. ground cumin
1 cup shredded sharp cheddar cheese

In a large sauce pan over medium heat, add the great northern beans with liquid, hominy with liquid, tomatoes with liquid, bean and bacon soup, tomatoes and green chiles with liquid, corn with liquid, water, bay leaves, cilantro and cumin. Stir until well combined.

Bring the soup to a boil. Once the soup is at a boil, reduce the heat to low and place a lid on the pan. Simmer for 30 minutes and remove the pan from the heat. Remove the bay leaves and discard. Spoon the soup into bowls and sprinkle the cheddar cheese over the top of each serving.

White Bean & Collard Green Soup

Makes 8 servings

4 bacon slices
2 cups chopped smoked ham
1 onion, finely chopped
6 cups cooked navy beans
1 cup barbecue sauce
6 oz. can tomato sauce
1 tbs. instant chicken bouillon granules
1 tsp. ground chipotle chile pepper
1/2 tsp. dried thyme
1/2 tsp. black pepper
8 cups water
3 cups shredded fresh collard greens
Tabasco sauce to taste

In a large dutch oven, add the bacon slices. Place the pot over medium heat and cook about 6 minutes or until the bacon is crisp. Remove the bacon from the pot and drain on paper towels. Crumble the bacon into pieces. Leave the bacon drippings in the pot.

Add the ham and onion to the bacon drippings. Stir frequently and cook for 10 minutes. Drain off the excess grease. Add the navy beans, barbecue sauce, tomato sauce, chicken bouillon, chipotle pepper, thyme, black pepper and water to the pot. Stir until combined and bring the soup to a boil. When the soup is boiling, reduce the heat to medium low and place a lid on the pot. Simmer the soup for 1 hour.

Stir in the collard greens and cook for 10 minutes. The collard greens should be tender. Remove the pot from the heat and serve. This is delicious with hot cornbread to sop up the juices. Season with Tabasco sauce to taste.

Navy Bean Squash Soup

Makes 12 servings

1 lb. dried navy beans, sorted and rinsed
3 3/4 cups chicken broth
Water
1 meaty ham bone
5 cups butternut squash, peeled and cubed
1 onion, chopped
1/2 tsp. salt
1/2 tsp. black pepper

In a dutch oven, add the navy beans. Cover the beans with water about 2" above the beans. Place the beans on the stove over high heat. Bring the beans to a boil and boil for 3 minutes. Remove the pot from the heat and place a lid on the pot. Let the beans soak for 3 hours at room temperature.

When the beans have soaked, drain all the water from the beans. Rinse the beans with cold water and drain the beans again. Add the chicken broth, 2 cups water, ham bone, butternut squash, onion, salt and black pepper to the beans. Place the pot back on the stove over medium heat. Bring the beans to a boil and place a lid on the pot. Reduce the heat to low and simmer for 2 hours or until the beans are tender.

Remove the ham bone from the beans. Cut any ham from the bone and add back to the beans. Remove the pot from the heat. Using a potato masher, mash the beans and squash. You do not have to mash the beans and squash and you can leave the beans and squash chunky if preferred. Spoon into bowls and serve.

Black, White & Red Soup

Makes a little over 5 cups

15 oz. can white hominy, rinsed and drained
15 oz. can black beans, rinsed and drained
14 oz. can chili style stewed tomatoes
14 oz. can chicken broth
1 tsp. minced fresh cilantro
1/2 tsp. chili powder
1/2 tsp. ground cumin

In a large sauce pan over medium heat, add the hominy, black beans, tomatoes with liquid, chicken broth, cilantro, chili powder and cumin. Stir until well combined. Stir frequently and cook for 10 minutes or until the soup is hot and the spices well combined when ready. Remove the soup from the heat and serve.

Spicy White Bean Soup

Makes about 12 cups

1 onion, chopped
2 tbs. melted unsalted butter
4 cups cooked great northern beans, rinsed and drained
4 cups cooked yellow hominy, rinsed and drained
2 cans chili style diced tomatoes, 14 oz. size
3 1/2 cups vegetable broth
1 tsp. granulated sugar
1/2 tsp. ground cumin
1/2 tsp. cayenne pepper
1/4 tsp. ground cloves
2 tbs. chopped fresh cilantro
Salt and black pepper to taste
Tabasco sauce to taste

In a dutch oven over medium heat, add the onion and butter. Saute the onion for 4 minutes. Add the great northern beans, hominy, tomatoes with juice, vegetable broth, granulated sugar, cumin, cayenne pepper, cloves and cilantro. Stir until well combined. Bring the soup to a boil. When the soup is boiling, reduce the heat to low. Simmer the soup for 20 minutes. Remove the pan from the heat and season with salt, black pepper and Tabasco sauce to taste. This soup freezes well.

Beanolla Soup

Makes 8 servings

1 lb. boneless pork chops, cubed
1 tbs. unsalted butter, melted
1 tbs. olive oil
2 onions, chopped
3 garlic cloves, minced
5 1/4 cups chicken broth
6 cups cooked pinto beans, rinsed and drained
1 1/4 tsp. dried oregano
3/4 tsp. cumin seeds
1/2 tsp. black pepper
Vegetable oil for frying
12 corn tortillas, 6" size
6 oz. cream cheese, cut into cubes
Diced tomatoes, optional
Sliced green onions, optional

In a large dutch oven over medium heat, add the pork, melted butter and olive oil. Cook until the pork is well browned and no longer pink. Remove the pork from the pan and drain on paper towels. Leave the drippings in the skillet.

Add the onions and garlic to the pan. Stir constantly and cook for 5 minutes. Add the pork back to the pan and stir in the chicken broth, pinto beans, oregano, cumin seeds and black pepper. Stir frequently and bring the soup to a boil. When the soup is boiling, place a lid on the pan and reduce the heat to low. Simmer the soup for 20 minutes. Remove the soup from the heat.

Cut the tortillas into 1/4" strips. In a skillet over medium heat, add the vegetable oil to a depth of 1" in the skillet. When the oil is hot, add the tortilla strips. Fry the strips until browned. You will need to fry the strips in 2-3 batches. Remove the strips when done and drain on paper towels.

Spoon the soup into bowls and top the soup with tortillas and cream cheese cubes. Sprinkle the tomatoes and green onions over the top if desired.

Lentil Vegetable Soup

Makes 8 servings

2 cups lentils
Water
2 slices bacon, diced
1/2 cup chopped onion
1/2 cup chopped celery
1/4 cup chopped carrots
3 tbs. fresh minced parsley
1 garlic clove, minced
2 1/2 tsp. salt
1/4 tsp. black pepper
1/2 tsp. dried oregano
16 oz. can petite diced tomatoes
2 tbs. wine vinegar

Rinse the lentils well with cold water. Place the lentils in a large sauce pan over medium heat. Add 8 cups water, bacon, onion, celery, carrots, parsley, garlic, salt, black pepper and oregano. Stir until well combined and bring the lentils to a boil. When the lentils are boiling, reduce the heat to low. Cover the sauce pan with a lid and cook about 1 1/2 hours or until the lentils are almost tender.

Add the tomatoes with liquid and vinegar to the pan. Stir until well combined. Simmer the soup for 30 minutes. Remove the pan from the heat and season with additional black pepper if desired.

Sausage Lentil Soup

Makes about 3 quarts

12 oz. dried lentils
2 carrots, sliced
2 onions, chopped
2 celery stalks, chopped
1 tbs. melted unsalted butter
1 lb. Polish sausage, sliced and cooked
8 oz. cooked ham, diced
1 bay leaf
1 tsp. dried thyme
2 whole cloves
1 tsp. granulated sugar
1 tsp. vinegar
1 tsp. tomato paste
1 pkg. brown gravy mix
Water
2 potatoes, peeled and cubed

Add the lentils to a large pot. Cover the lentils with cold water to about 1" above the lentils. Place a lid on the pot and soak the lentils overnight or about 12 hours. When the lentils have soaked, drain all the water from the lentils.

In a skillet over medium heat, add the carrots, onions, celery and butter. Saute the vegetables about 7 minutes. Remove the pan from the heat and add the vegetables to the lentils in the pot.

Add the Polish sausage, ham, bay leaf, thyme, cloves, granulated sugar, vinegar, tomato paste, brown gravy mix and 4 cups water to the pot. Stir until well combined and place the pot over medium heat. Bring the soup to a boil and reduce the heat to low. Place a lid on the pot and simmer for 20 minutes. Add the potatoes to the pot and simmer for 25 minutes or until the lentils and potatoes are tender. You can add additional water if you like for a thinner soup. Remove the soup from the heat and serve.

Navy Bean Soup with Ham Hocks

Makes 12 hearty servings

3 cups dried navy beans
Water
16 oz. can petite diced tomatoes
1 1/4 cups diced onion
1 lb. meaty ham hock
2 cups chicken broth
1/2 cup white wine
Salt and black pepper to taste

Add the navy beans to a large pot. Cover the beans with cold water about 2" above the beans. Place a lid on the pot and let the beans soak overnight or at least 12 hours. When the beans have soaked, drain off the soaking water and rinse the beans with cold water.

Add the tomatoes with juice, onion, ham hock, chicken broth and white wine to the pot. Add water if needed to cover the beans. Bring the beans to a boil over medium heat. When the beans are boiling, reduce the temperature to low and simmer the beans about 2 hours or until the beans are tender. Add water if needed to keep the beans covered while cooking.

Remove the ham hock and half of the beans from the pot. Place the beans in a blender and puree until the beans are smooth. Add the pureed beans back to the pot. Remove the meat from the ham hock and place the meat back in the pot with the beans. Season to taste with salt and black pepper. Remove the soup from the heat and serve.

Ham and Bean Soup

Makes 1 gallon

1 lb. dried great northern beans
Water
1 1/2 lbs. cubed cooked ham
2 tsp. salt
1 tsp. dried thyme
1/2 tsp. dried parsley flakes
4 peppercorns
3 garlic cloves, minced
1 bay leaf
4 potatoes, peeled and quartered
3 carrots, peeled and cut into 1/2" slices
1 onion, finely chopped

Rinse the beans with cold water and remove any bad beans. In a large pot, add the beans. Cover the beans with cold water about 3" above the beans. Place a lid on the pot and soak the beans overnight.

Drain the water from the beans. Rinse the beans with cold water and drain again. Add 6 cups water to the pot and place the pot over medium heat. Stir in the ham, salt, thyme, parsley, peppercorns, garlic and bay leaf. Stir until combined and bring the beans to a boil. When the beans are boiling, place a lid on the pot and simmer for 1 1/2 hours.

Add 2 cups water, potatoes, carrots and onion to the pot. Place the lid back on the pot and simmer about 30 minutes or until the beans and potatoes are tender. Remove the pan from the heat. Remove the bay leaf and discard.

Creamy Lentil Soup

Makes 5 servings

1 cup lentils
2 1/2 cups water
2 tsp. salt
1/4 tsp. black pepper
1 cup onion, finely chopped
1 garlic clove, minced
1/4 cup tomato sauce
1 bay leaf
1 1/2 cups whole milk

Rinse the lentils well with cold water and place in a large sauce pan. Add the water, salt, black pepper, onion, garlic, tomato sauce and bay leaf. Stir until well combined. Place the sauce pan over medium low heat. Cover the sauce pan with a lid and simmer the lentils about 1 hour or until the lentils are tender.

Remove the pan from the heat. Remove the bay leaf and discard. Pour the lentils and liquid into a blender. Puree until smooth. Pour the puree back into the sauce pan. Add the whole milk and stir until combined. Place the pan back on the stove and cook only until the soup is thoroughly heated. Do not let the soup boil or the boiling milk will ruin the soup.

Season to taste with additional salt and black pepper if desired. A dash of cayenne pepper or a few drops Tabasco sauce is great in this soup.

Ham Lentil Soup

Makes 2 quarts

1 lb. dried lentils
Water
5 beef bouillon cubes
1 onion, chopped
1 garlic clove, minced
1 carrot, chopped
1 celery stalk, chopped
1/4 tsp. dry mustard
1 cup diced cooked ham
Salt and black pepper to taste

Wash the lentils and place the lentils in a stock pot. Cover the lentils with 3 quarts cold water. Place a lid on the pot and let the lentils soak overnight. Do not drain the lentils.

Add the beef bouillon, onion, garlic, carrot, celery and dry mustard to the lentils. Place the pot over medium heat and bring the lentils to a boil. Place a lid on the pot and simmer the soup for 1 1/2 hours. Add the diced ham and simmer about 30 minutes or until the lentils are tender. Season to taste with salt and black pepper. Remove the pot from the heat and serve. You can leave the soup as is or puree half of the soup to make a creamy lentil soup.

Spinach Bean Soup

Makes 5 cups

1/2 cup chopped onion
1 garlic clove, minced
1 tbs. melted unsalted butter
1 1/4 cups chicken broth
1 1/3 cups water
4 cups fresh spinach, chopped
15 oz. can garbanzo beans
1/8 tsp. black pepper
2 tbs. grated Parmesan cheese

In a large sauce pan over medium heat, add the onion, garlic and butter. Saute the onion and garlic for 4 minutes. Add the chicken broth and water and bring the soup to a low boil. Simmer for 10 minutes.

Stir in the spinach, garbanzo beans with liquid and black pepper. Place a lid on the sauce pan and simmer for 5 minutes. Remove the soup from the heat and spoon the soup into serving bowls. Sprinkle the Parmesan cheese over the top of each bowl and serve.

Country Pea Soup

Makes 6 cups

1 lb. dried split peas
10 cups water
2 lbs. ham hocks
1 onion, chopped
1 stalk celery, chopped
1 garlic clove, minced
1/8 tsp. black pepper
Salt to taste

In a large pot, add the peas, water, ham hocks, onion, celery, garlic and black pepper. Stir to combine the ingredients. Place the pot over medium high heat and bring the soup to a boil. When the soup is boiling, reduce the heat to low. Place a lid on the pot and simmer about 1 hour or until the peas are tender.

Remove the ham hocks from the soup. Place 3 cups of the soup into a blender. Puree until smooth. Add the puree back to the pot. You can puree the rest of the soup if desired. I like a mixture of smooth and chunky soup. Remove the meat from the ham hocks and add to the soup. Season with salt to taste. Serve with hot cornbread, biscuits or crackers.

Hearty Bean and Barley Soup

Makes about 5 quarts

This makes a lot of soup so freeze the extra for quick dinners.

2 lbs. dried great northern beans
Water
1 cup fine barley
1 ham hock
1 lb. cooked ground beef
1 onion, chopped
8 garlic cloves, chopped
6 carrots, sliced
5 cups vegetable or chicken consomme
1 1/2 tsp. salt
1 tsp. black pepper
1/4 cup Worcestershire sauce
1/2 tsp. Tabasco sauce
2 jalapeno peppers, seeded and chopped

In a large dutch oven, add the great northern beans. Cover the beans with cold water about 3" above the beans. Cover the pot with a lid and let the beans soak at least 12 hours but no more than 24 hours. Drain all the water from the beans. Rinse the beans with cold water and drain again.

Add 2 quarts water, barley, ham hock, ground beef, onion, garlic, carrots, vegetable consomme, salt, black pepper, Worcestershire sauce, Tabasco sauce and the jalapeno peppers to the pot. Bring the beans to a boil. When the beans are at a full boil, reduce the heat to low. Place a lid on the pot and simmer about 3 hours. The beans should be tender and the soup slightly thickened. You may need to add a little more water to the beans while cooking. Keep the beans barely covered in water while cooking. Remove the soup from the heat.

Remove the ham hock from the soup. Cut the meat from the ham hock and add the meat to the soup if desired.

White Bean Pot

Makes a little over 3 quarts

2 cups dried great northern beans
Water
3/4 lb. diced cooked ham
4 carrots, peeled and diced
1 large tomato, peeled and chopped
1 large onion, chopped
3/4 cup minced fresh parsley
1/4 cup chopped celery
1 garlic clove, minced
1 bay leaf
3/4 tsp. salt
1/4 tsp. black pepper
1/4 tsp. paprika
1/8 tsp. dried thyme
1/8 tsp. dried marjoram
Pinch of ground cloves
1 tbs. melted unsalted butter
1 lb. cooked knockwurst, cut into 1/4" slices

Wash the beans with cold water and remove any bad beans. Add the beans to a large pot or dutch oven. Cover the beans with water about 1" above the beans. Place the beans on the stove over medium heat. Bring the beans to a full boil and boil the beans for 2 minutes. Turn the stove off and place a lid on the pot. Let the beans soak for 1 hour.

Place the beans back on the stove over medium heat and bring the beans to a boil. When the beans are boiling, reduce the heat to low. Simmer the beans for 1 hour. The beans should be almost tender.

Add the ham, carrots, tomato, onion, parsley, celery, garlic clove, bay leaf, salt, black pepper, paprika, thyme, marjoram and ground cloves to the pot. Stir until well combined. Add water as needed to cover the beans and vegetables with water. Bring the beans back to a boil and simmer about 30 minutes or until the beans and vegetables are tender.

When the beans are almost done, add butter to a skillet over medium heat. Add the knockwurst and saute the knockwurst until the slices are well browned. Remove the skillet from the heat and add the knockwurst to the beans. Cook for 10 minutes. Remove the soup from the heat and serve.

Bean Counter Soup

Makes 8 cups

1/2 cup finely chopped onion
2 garlic cloves, minced
1 tbs. olive oil
1 tomato, finely chopped
3 1/2 cups chicken broth
1 3/4 cups water
1/2 tsp. dried basil
1/2 tsp. dried oregano
1/2 tsp. dried celery flakes
6 cups cooked great northern beans
1 cup dry elbow macaroni
1/4 tsp. black pepper
1/2 cup grated Parmesan cheese

In a dutch oven, add the onion, garlic and olive oil. Stir constantly and saute the onion and garlic for 5 minutes. Add the tomato and simmer for 5 minutes. Stir in the chicken broth, water, basil, oregano and celery flakes. Bring the soup to a boil and reduce the heat to low. Simmer the soup for 5 minutes. Stir in the great northern beans, macaroni and black pepper. Stir occasionally and bring the soup back to a boil.

Stir occasionally and place a lid on the dutch oven. Simmer for 15 minutes or until the macaroni is tender. Remove the pot from the heat. Place the soup in serving bowls and sprinkle Parmesan cheese over each serving.

Ham and Black Eye Pea Stew

Makes 3 quarts

1 ham hock
1 lb. dried black eye peas
Water
1 onion, chopped
1 green bell pepper, chopped
3 celery stalks, chopped
1 1/2 lbs. cooked ham, cubed
1 bay leaf
2 tbs. ketchup
1 tbs. Worcestershire sauce
1/4 tsp. black pepper
1/4 tsp. Tabasco sauce
1/2 cup chopped fresh parsley
8 green onions, thinly sliced

In a small sauce pan over medium heat, add the ham hock. Cover the ham hock with water and bring the water to a boil. Cook for 3 minutes. Remove the sauce pan from the heat and drain all the water from the ham hock.

In a large dutch oven over medium heat, add the ham hock, black eye peas, 8 cups water, onion, green bell pepper, celery, ham and bay leaf. Bring the peas to a boil and reduce the heat to low. Simmer the peas for 1 to 1 1/2 hours or until the peas are tender. Stir the peas occasionally while they cook.

Add the ketchup, Worcestershire sauce, black pepper and Tabasco sauce to the pan. Stir until well combined. Simmer the peas for 15 minutes. Stir in the parsley and green onions. Simmer for 10 minutes. Remove the stew from the heat and serve. This stew freezes well.

2 PINTO BEANS

Pinto beans are my family's favorite bean. We eat them on a regular basis. These recipes will provide you casseroles, main dishes and side dishes for new ways to serve brown beans.

I cook my beans from dried beans in the slow cooker. I freeze the cooled beans in 2 cup increments. I thaw the beans overnight in the refrigerator so I can put together dinner in a hurry.

Navajo Tacos with Turkey Pinto Bean Topping

Makes 8 servings

1 cup dried pinto beans
Water
1 1/2 lbs. ground turkey
1 tbs. vegetable oil
2 tbs. chili powder
2 cups shredded American cheese
4 1/2 cups all purpose flour
2 tbs. nonfat dry milk powder
1 tbs. baking powder
1 tsp. salt
1 1/2 cups warm water
Vegetable oil for frying
3 cups shredded lettuce
2 large tomatoes, chopped
1 onion, finely chopped

In a large pot, add the pinto beans. Cover the beans with cold water about 2" above the beans. Place a lid on the pot and soak the beans at least 12 hours. Drain the water from the beans and rinse the beans with cold water.

Add 5 1/2 cups water to the beans in the pot. Bring the beans to a boil and reduce the heat to medium low. Simmer the beans about 1 to 1 1/2 hours or until the beans are tender. Remove the pot from the heat. Drain the liquid from the beans but save 1/4 cup bean liquid. Set the beans aside for now.

In a skillet over medium heat, add the ground turkey and 1 tablespoon vegetable oil. Stir frequently to break the turkey into crumbles as it cooks. Cook about 7 minutes or until the turkey is well browned and no longer pink. Stir in the beans, 1/4 cup bean liquid and chili powder. Stir until well combined. Stir in the American cheese and cook only until the cheese is melted. Remove the skillet from the heat.

When the turkey bean topping is almost ready, make the tacos. In a mixing bowl, add the all purpose flour, dry milk powder, baking powder and salt. Whisk until well combined. Slowly stir in 1 1/2 cups warm water. Stir until a stiff dough forms. Lightly flour your work surface. Turn the dough onto the work surface. Knead the dough for 5 minutes. The dough should be smooth and elastic when ready.

Navajo Tacos with Turkey Pinto Bean Topping cont'd

Divide the dough into 8 equal portions. Let the dough rest for 10 minutes. When the dough has rested, roll each portion to an 8" circle about 1/8" thick. In a deep skillet over high heat, add vegetable oil to a depth of 1" in the skillet. The temperature of the oil should be 400°. Cook one dough circle at a time. Drop the dough into the hot oil and cook about 1 minute on each side. The tacos should be puffed and golden brown when ready. Remove the tacos from the oil and drain on paper towels. Sprinkle the tacos with salt if desired.

To keep the tacos warm until all the tacos are done, place the fried tacos on a platter in a 200° oven. When ready to serve, place a taco on each serving plate. Spoon the turkey bean mixture over the taco. Sprinkle the lettuce, tomato and onion over the turkey bean mixture.

Skillet Veggie & Bean Tacos

Makes 12 servings

2 red bell peppers, chopped
1 onion, chopped
1 cup sliced fresh mushrooms
1 jalapeno pepper, seeded and chopped
2 tsp. olive oil
1 1/2 tsp. ground cumin
1 tsp. dried oregano
3/4 cup sweet white wine
2 cups cooked pinto beans
2 cups chopped fresh spinach
12 flour tortillas, 8" size, warmed
1/2 cup crumbled feta cheese, optional

In a large skillet over medium high heat, add the red bell peppers, onion, mushrooms, jalapeno pepper and olive oil. Saute the vegetables about 5 minutes. Stir in the cumin and oregano and cook for 2 minutes.

Reduce the heat to medium low and stir in the white wine. Simmer about 10 minutes or until the liquid is reduced by about half. Stir in the pinto beans and cook only until heated. Stir in the spinach and cook for 2 minutes. Remove the skillet from the heat. Spoon the mixture into the tortillas and sprinkle the feta cheese over the top if desired.

Chicken and Bean Tacos

Makes 8 tacos

8 flour tortillas, 8" size
2/3 cup chopped onion
1/3 cup chopped green bell pepper
2 tbs. vegetable oil
2 cups shredded cooked chicken
16 oz. jar taco sauce
1 tsp. granulated sugar
1 1/2 tsp. chili powder
15 oz. can refried beans
8 taco shells, heated crisp
2 cups shredded lettuce
1 cup chopped tomato
1 cup shredded cheddar cheese

Warm the tortillas and place in a tortilla warmer or aluminum foil to keep them soft and warm. In a skillet over medium heat, add the onion, green bell pepper and vegetable oil. Saute the onion and green pepper for 4 minutes. Stir in the chicken, taco sauce, granulated sugar and chili powder. Stir constantly and cook for 1 minute or until the mixture is thoroughly heated. Remove the skillet from the heat.

Heat the refried beans in the microwave or in a sauce pan. Only cook until the beans are thoroughly heated. Spread 2 tablespoons refried beans on each flour tortilla. Place a taco shell in the center of the tortilla. Press the flour tortilla up the sides of the taco shell.

Fill each taco with 1/4 cup lettuce, 1/3 cup chicken mixture, 2 tablespoons tomato and 2 tablespoons cheddar cheese. Serve immediately.

Spicy Bean Enchiladas

Makes 8 servings

12 oz. dried pinto beans
Water
3 garlic cloves, minced
3/4 tsp. salt
1 bay leaf
2 cups tomato sauce
4 oz. can diced green chiles
3/4 cup plus 2 tbs. chopped green onion
2 1/2 tsp. chili powder
1 tsp. ground cumin
1/4 tsp. dried oregano
1/4 tsp. black pepper
8 corn tortillas, 6" size
1 cup shredded cheddar cheese
1/2 cup sour cream

Rinse the beans with cold water and remove any bad beans. Add the beans to a large pot and add cold water to about 2" above the beans. Soak the beans for 8-12 hours. When the beans have soaked, drain all the water from the beans. Rinse the beans with cold water and drain again. Add the beans, 8 cups water, 2 garlic cloves, salt and bay leaf to the pot. Bring the beans to a boil over medium heat. When the beans are boiling, place a lid on the pot and reduce the heat to low. Simmer the beans for 1 1/2 to 2 hours or until the beans are tender. Remove the pot from the heat. Drain all the water from the beans and discard the bay leaf.

While the beans are cooking, make the sauce. In a sauce pan over medium heat, add the tomato sauce, green chiles, 1 garlic clove, 3/4 cup green onions, 2 teaspoons chili powder, cumin and oregano. Stir constantly and bring the sauce to a boil. Reduce the heat to low and simmer for 5 minutes. Remove the sauce from the heat.

Using a potato masher or a fork, mash the beans. The beans should still be chunky but not smooth like mashed potatoes. Stir in 1/2 cup of the sauce, 1/2 teaspoon chili powder and black pepper. Spray a 9 x 13 casserole dish with non stick cooking spray. Preheat the oven to 350°. Spoon 1/2 cup of the bean mixture in the center of each corn tortilla. Roll the tortillas up and place in the baking dish with the seam side down. Spoon the remaining sauce over the tortillas. Bake for 20 minutes. Sprinkle the cheddar cheese over the top of the dish. Bake for 5 minutes. Remove the dish from the oven and let the enchiladas rest for 5 minutes. Spoon the sour cream over the top of the dish. Sprinkle 2 tablespoons green onion over the top before serving.

Three Bean Enchiladas

Makes 12 servings

1/2 cup dried kidney beans
1/2 cup dried navy beans
1/2 cup dried pinto beans
Water
3/4 tsp. salt
1/2 cup chopped onion
2 garlic cloves
1 tsp. chili powder
1 tsp. ground cumin
4 oz. can diced green chiles
12 corn tortillas, 6" size
10 oz. can enchilada sauce
1 cup shredded Monterey Jack cheese

Rinse the beans in cold water and remove any bad beans. Place all the beans in a stock pot or dutch oven. Cover the beans with water about 2" above the beans. Place the pot over medium heat and bring the beans to a boil. Boil the beans for 2 minutes. Remove the pot from the heat and place a lid on the pot. Let the beans soak for 1 hour.

When the beans have soaked, drain all the water from the beans. Add 6 cups water and 1/2 teaspoon salt to the beans. Place the beans on the stove over medium heat and bring the beans to a boil. Place a lid on the pot and reduce the heat to low. Simmer the beans for 1 to 1 1/2 hours or until the beans are tender.

Remove the beans from the heat and drain off the bean liquid. You need to keep 1/4 cup bean liquid in a measuring cup. Add the beans, 1/4 cup bean liquid, onion, garlic, chili powder, cumin, 1/4 teaspoon salt and green chiles to a blender or food processor. Process until the mixture is chunky.

Spray a 9 x 13 baking dish with non stick cooking spray. Preheat the oven to 350°. Brush the tortillas with water to soften the tortillas. Spoon the bean mixture down the center of each tortilla. Roll each tortilla up and place the tortillas, seam side down, in the prepared dish. Pour the enchilada sauce over the tortillas. Place a lid on the dish or cover the dish with aluminum foil. Bake for 20 minutes. Remove the aluminum foil or lid from the pan. Sprinkle the Monterey Jack cheese over the top. Bake for 5 minutes. Remove the dish from the oven and cool for 5 minutes before serving.

Ranch Chili & Beans

Makes 8 servings

3 lbs. ground beef
6 cups water
2 bay leaves
8 garlic cloves, crushed
4 tbs. chili powder
2 tsp. salt
1 tsp. ground cumin
1 tsp. dried oregano
1/4 tsp. black pepper
1/4 tsp. cayenne pepper
2 tbs. paprika
1 tbs. granulated sugar
2 cans ranch style beans, 15 oz. size

In a large dutch oven over medium heat, add the ground beef. Stir frequently to break the ground beef into crumbles as it cooks. Cook about 10 minutes or until the ground beef is well browned and no longer pink. Drain off the excess grease.

Add the water, bay leaves and garlic to the ground beef. Reduce the heat to low and place a lid on the pot. Simmer for 1 hour. Stir in the chili powder, salt, cumin, oregano, black pepper, cayenne pepper, paprika and granulated sugar. Stir frequently and simmer for 30 minutes. Stir in the beans and simmer for 15 minutes. Remove the bay leaves and discard. Remove the pot from the heat and serve. Serve with hot buttered cornbread. For spicier chili, use additional chili powder and cayenne pepper to your taste.

Southwestern Beans

Makes 8 servings

1 lb. dried pinto beans
Water
1 meaty ham bone
2 onions, chopped
1 green bell pepper, chopped
3 garlic cloves, minced
10 oz. can diced tomatoes with green chiles
2 tsp. light brown sugar
1 tsp. salt
1 tsp. chili powder
1 tsp. dried basil
1 tsp. dried oregano
1 tsp. Worcestershire sauce
1/2 tsp. black pepper
1/2 tsp. dried thyme
1/2 tsp. dry mustard
1/8 tsp. cayenne pepper
2 bay leaves

Rinse the beans with cold water and remove any bad beans. Add the beans to a large pot. Cover the beans with cold water about 2" above the beans. Place the pot over medium high heat and bring the beans to a boil. Boil the beans for 2 minutes. Remove the pot from the heat and let the beans soak for 1 hour.

Drain all the water from the beans. Add 6 cups water, ham bone, onions, green bell pepper, garlic, tomatoes with juice, brown sugar, salt, chili powder, basil, oregano, Worcestershire sauce, black pepper, thyme, mustard, cayenne pepper and bay leaves to the beans. Stir until well combined.

Place the beans over high heat and bring the beans to a boil. When the beans are at a full boil, reduce the heat to medium low. Place a lid on the pot and simmer the beans about 2 to 2 1/2 hours or until the beans are tender. Remove the pot from the heat. Remove the ham bone and bay leaves. Cut the ham from the bone and add back to the beans if desired. Discard the bay leaves.

Spicy Hot Beans

Makes 10 servings

1 lb. pkg. dried pinto beans
Water
1 lb. bacon, cut into 1/2" pieces
1 lb. smoked link sausage, cut into 1/2" slices
2 onions, chopped
1/2 cup chopped green bell pepper
4 garlic cloves, minced
1/4 cup Worcestershire sauce
1/4 cup light brown sugar
2 tbs. ground cumin
1 tbs. chili powder
1 tbs. black pepper
1 tbs. celery seeds
2 tsp. Tabasco sauce
1 bay leaf
16 oz. can diced tomatoes with juice

Rinse the beans with cold water and remove any bad beans. Add the beans to a large pot. Cover the beans with cold water about 2" above the beans. Soak the beans for 12 hours. When the beans have soaked, drain all the water from the beans.

In a large skillet over medium heat, add the bacon, smoked sausage, onions, green bell pepper and garlic. Cook until the bacon is crisp and the vegetables tender. Remove the skillet from the heat and drain off the excess grease. Add the bacon, smoked sausage and vegetables to the beans.

Add 6 cups water, Worcestershire sauce, brown sugar, cumin, chili powder, black pepper, celery seeds, Tabasco sauce and bay leaf to the beans. Bring the beans to a boil over high heat. When the beans are boiling, reduce the heat to medium low. Place a lid on the pot and simmer the beans for 2 hours or until the beans are almost done. Stir in the tomatoes and simmer for 30 minutes. Remove the pot from the heat.

Mexican Pinto Beans

Makes 7 cups

1 lb. dried pinto beans
Water
6 bacon slices, finely chopped
1/2 cup green bell pepper, chopped
1 1/2 tbs. ground cumin
1 tbs. chili powder
1 1/2 tsp. salt
1 tsp. black pepper

Rinse the pinto beans with cold water and remove any bad beans. Place the beans in a dutch oven. Cover the beans with water to about 2" above the beans. Place the beans on the stove over medium heat. Bring the beans to a boil and boil for 3 minutes. Remove the beans from the heat and place a lid on the pan. Let the beans soak for 1 hour.

When the beans have soaked, drain all the water from the beans. Add 5 cups water, bacon, green bell pepper, cumin, chili powder, salt and black pepper. Stir until combined. Place the beans back over medium heat and bring the beans to a boil. When the beans are boiling, place the lid back on the pan and reduce the heat to medium low. Simmer the beans for 1 1/2 - 2 hours or until the beans are tender. Remove the pan from the heat and serve. I like to drain the beans and remove the bacon before serving.

Pinto Beans with Spareribs

Makes 6 servings

1 lb. dried pinto beans, washed
Water
3 lbs. pork spareribs
Salt, black pepper and chili powder to taste
2 green bell peppers, cut into quarters
2 onions, sliced
29 oz. can diced tomatoes

In a stock pot over medium heat, add the dried pinto beans. Cover the beans with cold water. Bring the beans to a boil and boil for 3 minutes. Remove the pot from the heat. Place a lid on the pot and let the beans soak for 1 hour.

While the beans are soaking, cut the spareribs into serving size pieces. In a large skillet or dutch oven over medium heat, add the spareribs. Brown the ribs about 10 minutes or until well browned. Cover the ribs with water and place a lid on the skillet. Simmer the ribs about 45 minutes or until the ribs are tender. Remove the skillet from the heat.

Preheat the oven to 325°. Drain the beans and place in a roasting pan. Place the spareribs over the beans. Pour the water from the spareribs over the beans. Season to taste with salt, black pepper and chili powder.

Place the green bell peppers and onions over the beans and ribs. Pour the tomatoes with any juice over the top of the ribs. Cover the pan with aluminum foil or a lid. Bake for 1 to 1 1/2 hours or until the beans are tender. Remove the pan from the oven and serve.

Hearty Pinto Beans with Sausage

Makes about 5 quarts

This recipe freezes well or feeds a huge crowd.

2 lbs. dried pinto beans
3 smoked ham hocks, about 6 oz. each
1 large onion, chopped
1 garlic clove, minced
3 tbs. hot chili powder
2 tsp. salt
1 tsp. ground cumin
1/2 tsp. dried oregano
Water
1 lb. fresh chorizo sausage

Rinse the beans with cold water and remove any bad beans. Place the beans in a large stock pot. Cover the beans with water about 2" above the beans. Soak the beans for 12 hours. When the beans have soaked, drain all the water from the beans. Rinse the beans with cold water and drain the beans again.

Add the ham hocks, onion, garlic, chili powder, salt, cumin, oregano and 3 1/2 quarts water to the beans in the pot. Place the beans over high heat and bring the beans to a boil. When the beans are boiling, reduce the heat to medium low. Place a lid on the pot and simmer the beans for 2 to 2 1/2 hours. The beans should be almost tender at this point.

Remove the casing from the chorizo sausage. Cut the chorizo into 1" slices and add to the beans. Simmer the beans and sausage about 1 hour or until the beans are tender and the sausage done. Remove the pot from the heat and serve.

Easy Bean and Cheese Chimichangas

Makes 4 servings

32 oz. can refried beans
2 cups shredded Monterey Jack cheese
2/3 cup salsa
2 tbs. taco seasoning mix
8 flour tortillas, 10" size
5 oz. pkg yellow rice mix, prepared
3 cups vegetable oil
Sour cream, optional

In a mixing bowl, add the refried beans, Monterey Jack cheese, salsa and taco seasoning mix. Stir until well combined. Spoon 1/3 cup of the mixture down the center of each tortilla. Spoon the the rice over the filling or serve the rice as a side dish.

Fold opposite sides of the tortillas over the filling forming a sealed rectangle. Secure the tortilla with toothpicks if desired. In a large skillet, add the vegetable oil. Heat the oil over medium heat to 325°. Fry each chimichanga about 4 minutes on each side. The chimichangas should be well browned. Remove the chimichangas from the skillet and drain on paper towels. Serve with sour cream if desired.

Ranch House Beans

Makes 10 servings

4 cups dried pinto beans
8 cups water
1/2 lb. salt pork
2-4 tbs. chili powder
1/4 tsp. Tabasco sauce
Salt to taste

In a stock pot over medium heat, add the beans and water. Bring the beans to a boil and boil for 2 minutes. Remove the beans from the heat. Place a lid on the pot and let the beans soak for 1 hour. Add the salt pork to the pot. Place the beans back on the stove over medium heat and bring the beans to a boil. When the beans are at a full boil, reduce the heat to medium low. Place a lid on the pot and simmer the beans for 2 hours or until the beans are tender. Stir in 2 tablespoons chili powder, Tabasco sauce and salt to taste. Add additional chili powder if desired. Simmer the beans for 2 minutes after adding the spices. Remove the beans from the heat and let the beans rest for 5 minutes before serving.

Razorback Beans

Makes 8 servings

1 lb. dried pinto beans
Water
1 lb. ground beef
1 onion, chopped
16 oz. can diced tomatoes
4 oz. can diced green chiles, drained
1/2 cup taco sauce
1 tsp. salt
1/2 tsp. chili powder
1/2 tsp. cumin seeds
1/2 tsp. dried oregano
1/2 tsp. garlic salt
1/2 tsp. black pepper

In a stock pot over medium heat, add the beans. Cover the beans with cold water about 2" above the beans. Bring the beans to a boil and boil for 2 minutes. Remove the beans from the heat. Place a lid on the pot and let the beans sit for 1 hour.

Drain the beans and cover the beans with fresh cold water. Bring the beans to a boil over medium heat. When the beans are boiling, reduce the heat to low and place a lid on the pot. Simmer the beans for 1 1/2 hours or until the beans are tender. Remove the pan from the heat. Drain the liquid from the beans but reserve 2 cups bean liquid for use later in the recipe.

In a skillet over medium heat, add the ground beef and onion. Stir the ground beef frequently to break the meat into crumbles as it cooks. Cook about 7 minutes or until the ground beef is browned and no longer pink. Remove the skillet from the heat and drain the excess grease from the skillet.

Add the ground beef and onion to the beans. Add 2 cups reserved bean liquid, tomatoes with juice, green chiles, taco sauce, salt, chili powder, cumin seeds, oregano, garlic salt and black pepper. Stir until well combined. Place the pot back over low heat. Place a lid on the pot and simmer about 1 hour. Add water if needed to keep the beans covered while cooking. Remove the pot from the heat and serve.

Pinto Bean Chalupas

Makes 12 servings

1 lb. dried pinto beans
Water
3 lb. boneless pork or beef roast
2 garlic cloves, minced
2 large onions, chopped
2 tbs. chili powder
1 tbs. ground cumin
1 tsp. salt
4 oz. can chopped green chiles
1 tsp. dried oregano
15 oz. pkg. corn chips
1 head iceberg lettuce, shredded
3 large tomatoes, peeled and chopped
3 cups shredded sharp cheddar cheese
16 oz. bottle taco sauce

Rinse the pinto beans with cold water. Remove any bad beans. In a large dutch oven, add the beans. Cover the beans with cold water. Add the boneless pork or beef, garlic, onions, chili powder, cumin, salt and green chiles to the pot. Place the pot over medium heat and bring the beans to a boil.

Reduce the heat to low and place a lid on the pot. Simmer the beans and meat about 3 hours or until the beans and meat are tender. Add water if needed to keep the beans covered in water. Stir in the oregano and leave the lid off the pot. Simmer for 30 minutes. Remove the pot from the heat.

Remove the meat from the pot. Shred the meat and add the shredded meat back to the pot. For each serving, place the corn chips in a single serving bowl. Spoon the meat and beans over the corn chips. Top each serving with lettuce, tomatoes, cheddar cheese and taco sauce.

Bean Burrito Appetizers

Makes 40 appetizers

1/2 cup chopped onion
15 oz. can pinto beans, drained and mashed
1/3 cup mild salsa
1 tbs. chili powder
1/8 tsp. garlic powder
1/8 tsp. salt
1/8 tsp. black pepper
1/4 cup cream cheese, softened
1/2 cup cubed avocado
1 1/2 tsp. lemon juice
10 flour tortillas, 6" size
1 red bell pepper, cut into thin strips
Salsa and sour cream, optional

Spray a skillet with non stick cooking spray. Add the onion and saute the onion for 4 minutes. Stir in the mashed pinto beans, salsa, chili powder, garlic powder, salt and black pepper. Remove the skillet from the heat and set aside for the moment.

In a small bowl, add the cream cheese, avocado and lemon juice. Stir until combined. Spread the mixture on 1 side of each tortilla. Spread 2 tablespoons bean mixture over the cream cheese spread. Top each tortilla with the red bell pepper strips. Roll the tortilla up. Cut each tortilla into fourths. Serve the tortillas with salsa and sour cream if desired.

Easy Cheesy Smoked Sausage with Beans Casserole

Makes 12 servings

1 lb. ground chuck
1 green bell pepper, diced
1 large onion, chopped
1 lb. smoked sausage, sliced
2 cans condensed tomato soup, 10.75 size
10 oz. can diced tomatoes with green chiles
8 cups cooked pinto beans
4 cans pork and beans, 15 oz. size
1/2 tsp. salt
1/2 tsp. black pepper
2 cups shredded cheddar cheese

In a skillet over medium heat, add the ground chuck, green bell pepper and onion. Stir frequently to break the ground chuck into crumbles as the meat cooks. Cook about 6 minutes or until the ground chuck is browned and no longer pink. Remove the skillet from the heat and drain off the excess grease.

In a large stock pot over medium heat, add the smoked sausage. Saute the sausage about 5 minutes or until the sausage is well browned. Add the ground chuck, tomato soup, diced tomatoes with green chiles including the juice, pinto beans, pork and beans with liquid, salt and black pepper to the pot. Stir until well combined.

Bring the beans to a boil. When the beans are boiling, reduce the heat to low. Stir occasionally and simmer for 30 minutes. Stir in the cheddar cheese. Remove the pot from the heat and serve.

Sweet Hot Pinto Beans

Makes 8 servings

1 lb. dried pinto beans
Water
3 dried red chiles, washed and seeded
4 slices bacon, chopped
2 tsp. salt
1 large onion, quartered
1 green bell pepper, chopped
1/4 cup light brown sugar

In a dutch oven, add the pinto beans. Cover the beans with cold water about 3" above the beans. Place the lid on the pot and soak the beans overnight or at least 12 hours.

When the beans have soaked, drain all the water from the beans. Rinse the beans with cold water and drain again. Add the red chiles, bacon and salt to the beans. Cover the beans with cold water about 1" above the beans. Place the beans on the stove over medium heat and bring the beans to a rolling boil. When the beans are boiling, reduce the heat to low. Place a lid on the pot and simmer for 2-3 hours or until the beans are tender. Make sure the heat is high enough to keep the beans at a low simmer.

Add the onion, green bell pepper and brown sugar to the beans. Stir until combined and simmer the beans for 30 minutes. Remove the beans from the heat and serve.

Frijoles Rancheros

Makes 6 servings

1 1/2 cups dried pinto beans
6 cups water
1/2 cup chopped lean cooked ham
2/3 cup plus 1/2 cup chopped onion
1/2 tsp. black pepper
1/2 tsp. crushed red pepper flakes
1 tbs. minced garlic
2 bay leaves
1 1/2 cups chopped tomato
1 tsp. dried oregano
1 tbs. Worcestershire sauce

Rinse the beans with cold water and remove any bad beans. Add the beans and water to a large pot. Place the pot on the stove over medium high heat and bring the beans to a boil. When the beans are at a full boil, boil for 3 minutes. Remove the pot from the heat. Place a lid on the pot and let the beans soak for 1 hour.

When the beans have soaked for 1 hour, add the ham, 2/3 cup onion, black pepper, red pepper flakes, garlic and bay leaves to the pot. Place the pot on the stove over medium heat. Stir frequently and simmer the beans for 1 1/2 to 2 hours or until the beans are tender. Remove the pot from the heat. Remove the bay leaves and discard.

While the beans are cooling, make the sauce for the beans. Spray a 10" skillet with non stick cooking spray. Add 1/2 cup onion to the skillet and place the skillet over medium heat. Saute the onion for 4 minutes. Stir in the tomato and oregano. Stir frequently and cook for 3 minutes. Add the Worcestershire sauce and stir until well combined. Remove the skillet from the heat. When ready to serve, spoon the beans into a bowl and serve the sauce over the beans.

Pinto Bean Enchilada Stack

Makes 6 servings

1 lb. lean ground chuck
1 envelope taco seasoning mix
1/3 cup water
16 oz. can refried beans
15 oz. can pinto beans, drained and rinsed
5 flour tortillas, 10" size
2 1/2 cups shredded Mexican cheese blend
10 oz. can enchilada sauce
Sour cream, tomatoes, green onions and black olives, optional

Preheat the oven to 425°. In a skillet over medium heat, add the ground chuck. Stir frequently to break the meat into crumbles as it cooks. Cook about 7 minutes or until the ground chuck is done and no longer pink. Remove the skillet from the heat and drain off any excess grease.

Stir in the taco seasoning mix and water. Stir frequently and cook for 2 minutes. Remove the skillet from the heat. In a mixing bowl, stir together the refried beans and pinto beans. Spray a jelly roll pan with non stick cooking spray. Place one tortilla on the baking pan. Spoon half of the ground chuck over the tortilla. Sprinkle 1/2 cup Mexican cheese over the ground chuck.

Place a tortilla over the cheese. Spoon half of the refried beans over the tortilla. Spoon half of the enchilada sauce over the beans. Sprinkle 1/2 cup cheese over the top. Place another tortilla on top of the cheese. Spoon the remaining ground chuck and 1/2 cup cheese over the tortilla. Place another tortilla on top of the ground beef. Spoon the remaining beans over the tortilla. Spoon the remaining enchilada sauce over the beans and sprinkle 1/2 cup cheese over the sauce.

Place the remaining tortilla on top. Bake for 15-17 minutes. The top tortilla should be lightly browned and the dish hot when ready. Sprinkle the remaining 1/2 cup cheese over the top. Bake for 3 minutes. Remove the dish from the oven and cool for 5 minutes before serving.

Picante Bean Sauce

Makes 2 1/2 cups

15 oz. can chili beans, drained
1 cup chunky picante sauce
1/4 cup chopped fresh cilantro
Hot cooked orzo or rice

In a sauce pan over medium heat, add the chili beans and picante sauce. Stir until combined. Cook about 5 minutes or until the beans and picante sauce come to a boil. Remove the pan from the heat and stir in the cilantro. Spoon the sauce over hot cooked pasta or rice. Sprinkle with your favorite cheese if desired.

Chili Bean Dip

I love this dip for games or when unexpected company drops by. It can be made in 5 minutes.

Makes 1 cup

15 oz. can chili beans
1/2 tsp. ground cumin
1/2 tsp. chili powder
1/4 tsp. dried oregano

Drain the beans but reserve 2 tablespoons bean liquid. Add the beans, 2 tablespoons bean liquid, cumin, chili powder and oregano to a blender. Process until the beans are mostly chopped but still slightly chunky.

Spoon the dip into a sauce pan over low heat. Stir constantly and cook only until the dip is hot. Remove the pan from the heat. Spoon the dip into a bowl and serve.

Prairie Fire Bean Dip

Makes 2 cups

16 oz. can refried beans
1 cup shredded provolone cheese
2/3 cup water
1/4 cup unsalted butter
2 tbs. minced onion
2 garlic cloves, minced
1 tbs. plus 1 tsp. chili powder
1/8 tsp. Tabasco sauce

Add all the ingredients to a sauce pan over low heat. Stir constantly until the butter and provolone cheese melt. The dip should be thoroughly heated when ready. Remove the pan from the heat and pour the dip into a serving bowl.

Serve with tortilla chips or fresh vegetables. My family loves to make bean burritos from this dip. Sprinkle additional cheese, chopped green onions and black olives over the beans in the tortilla. Serve with your favorite salsa or taco sauce if desired.

Pinto Bean Pie

Makes a 9" pie

1 1/2 cups granulated sugar
1 tsp. ground allspice
1 tsp. ground cinnamon
1 tsp. ground nutmeg
1 1/2 cups cooked, mashed pinto beans
1 egg, beaten
2 egg yolks, beaten
1 tsp. vanilla extract
Unbaked 9" pie crust, prepared

Preheat the oven to 350°. In a mixing bowl, add the granulated sugar, allspice, cinnamon and nutmeg. Whisk until well combined. Stir in the beans, egg, egg yolks and vanilla extract. Whisk until well combined. Pour the mixture into the prepared pie crust. Bake the pie for 15 minutes. Reduce the oven temperature to 300° and bake for 35-45 minutes. The pie should be set when ready. Remove the pie from the oven and cool completely before serving.

3 KIDNEY BEANS

I try to feed my family kidney beans at least once a week. Being from the south, we love red beans and rice. I have included numerous ways to prepare kidney beans.

Bean & Mushroom Burritos

Makes 8 servings

4 1/2 cups sliced fresh mushrooms
1 cup chopped onion
1 cup chopped green bell pepper
2 garlic cloves, crushed
2 tsp. olive oil
15 oz. can kidney beans, drained
2 tbs. finely chopped black olives
1/4 tsp. black pepper
Salt to taste
8 flour tortillas, 8" size
1/2 cup sour cream
1 cup salsa
1/2 cup shredded cheddar cheese

In a skillet over medium heat, add the mushrooms, onion, green bell pepper, garlic and olive oil. Stir frequently and saute the vegetables about 6 minutes or until the vegetables are tender. Stir in the kidney beans, black olives and black pepper. Stir constantly and bring the mixture to a boil. Remove the skillet from the heat and season with salt to taste.

Spoon 1/2 cup bean and vegetable mixture down the center of each tortilla. Top each burrito with 1 tablespoon sour cream, 1 tablespoon salsa and 1 tablespoon cheddar cheese. Fold the sides over the filling to form a burrito.

Spray a large skillet with non stick cooking spray. Place the skillet on the stove over medium heat. Place the burritos, seam side down, in the skillet. Cook about 1 minute on each side or until the burritos are thoroughly heated. Remove the burritos from the skillet and serve with the remaining salsa if desired.

Baked Bean Medley

Makes 12 servings

1 1/2 lbs. ground beef
1 onion, chopped
1 tsp. salt
15 oz. can kidney beans, drained
15 oz. can lima beans, drained
16 oz. can pork and beans
1/2 cup ketchup
1/4 cup light brown sugar
2 tbs. vinegar

In a skillet over medium heat, add the ground beef, onion and salt. Stir frequently to break the ground beef into crumbles as it cooks. Cook about 6-7 minutes or until the ground beef is well browned and no longer pink. Remove the pan from the heat and drain off the excess grease.

Preheat the oven to 350°. Spray a 3 quart casserole dish with non stick cooking spray. Add the ground beef, kidney beans, lima beans, pork and beans with liquid, ketchup, brown sugar and vinegar to the casserole dish. Stir until well combined. Bake for 30 minutes or until the beans are hot, bubbly and most of the liquid absorbed. Remove the dish from the oven and serve.

Hot Bean Dish

Makes 8 servings

5 cups cooked kidney beans
2 tsp. dry mustard
1 red chile pepper, minced
Pinch of cayenne pepper
2 garlic cloves, minced
1 onion, minced
1/4 cup bacon grease
1/2 cup sweet pickle juice
2 tbs. vinegar
1/4 cup strong coffee
6 slices bacon

Preheat the oven to 350°. In a 2 quart casserole dish, add the kidney beans, dry mustard, chile pepper, cayenne pepper, garlic, onion, bacon grease, pickle juice, vinegar and coffee. Stir until well combined. Bake for 30 minutes.

While the beans are cooking, add the bacon to a skillet. Cook the bacon over medium heat until the bacon is almost crispy. Place the bacon over the beans and cook for 15 minutes. The beans should be hot, bubbly and most of the liquid absorbed. Remove the dish from the oven and let the beans cool for 5 minutes before serving.

Vegetarian Saute'

Makes 4 servings

1 onion, chopped
1 green bell pepper, chopped
1 zucchini, chopped
2 garlic cloves, minced
2 tbs. olive oil
14 oz. can chili style stewed tomatoes
15 oz. can dark red kidney beans, drained
1/2 tsp. dried oregano
1/4 tsp. salt
1/4 tsp. black pepper
1/2 cup shredded cheddar cheese, optional

In a large skillet over medium heat, add the onion, green bell pepper, zucchini, garlic and olive oil. Saute the vegetables for 7 minutes or until the vegetables are tender. Stir in the tomatoes with juice, kidney beans, oregano, salt and black pepper. Stir frequently and cook for 5 minutes. Remove the skillet from the heat and sprinkle the cheddar cheese over the top if desired.

Kidney Bean Casserole

Makes 8 servings

1/2 cup unsalted butter
2 onions, chopped
2 green bell peppers, chopped
1/2 cup celery, chopped
8 cups cooked kidney beans
1 cup salsa
2 cans Rotel tomatoes, 10 oz. size
2 cups grated American cheese
6 cups hot cooked rice

Preheat the oven to 300°. In a skillet over medium heat, add the butter, onions, green bell peppers and celery. Saute the vegetables for 4-5 minutes or until the vegetables have softened. Add the kidney beans, salsa and Rotel tomatoes with liquid. Stir until well combined. Simmer for 10 minutes and remove the skillet from the heat.

Pour the mixture into a 3 quart casserole dish. Sprinkle the American cheese over the top of the casserole. Cover the dish with a lid or aluminum foil. Bake for 45 minutes. Remove the casserole from the oven . Place the rice on a serving platter. Spoon the casserole over the rice and serve.

Caribbean Beans & Rice

Makes 6 servings

1 cup dried kidney beans
Water
1/2 lb. salt pork
14 oz. can coconut milk
1 1/2 cups long grain rice
1/2 habanero chile, seeded and minced
1 garlic clove, minced
1 tsp. dried thyme
1 tsp. black pepper
1/2 tsp. salt
3 green onions, chopped

Place the kidney beans in a large dutch oven. Cover the beans with water about 2" above the beans. Place a lid on the pot and soak the beans for 12 hours. When the beans have soaked, drain all the water from the beans. Rinse the beans with cold water and drain the beans again.

Add the salt pork, 4 1/2 cups water and coconut milk to the beans. Place the pot over medium high heat and bring the beans to a boil. When the beans are boiling, reduce the heat to medium low. Place a lid on the pot and simmer the beans about 1 to 1 1/2 hours or until the beans are tender.

Stir in the rice, habanero chile, garlic, thyme, black pepper and salt. Bring the beans back to a boil and reduce the heat to low. Simmer for 25 minutes or until the rice is tender. Remove the pot from the heat. Remove the salt pork from the beans and discard. Sprinkle the green onions over the top of the dish before serving.

You can substitute 2 teaspoons Tabasco sauce for the habanero pepper if desired.

Creole Beans and Rice

Makes 12 servings

1 lb. dried red beans
Water
1/2 lb. salt pork
3 cups chopped onion
1 cup chopped fresh parsley
1 cup chopped green bell pepper
2 garlic cloves, finely minced
1 tbs. salt
1 tsp. cayenne pepper
1 tsp. black pepper
3 drops Tabasco sauce
1 tbs. Worcestershire sauce
8 oz. can tomato sauce
1/4 tsp. dried oregano
1/4 tsp. dried thyme
1 lb. German style sausage, cut into bite size pieces
6 cups hot cooked rice

Wash the beans and remove any bad beans. Place the beans in a large pot. Cover the beans with cold water about 3" above the beans. Place a lid on the pot and soak the beans at least 12 hours.

Drain all the water from the beans and rinse the beans with cold water. Place the beans back in the pot. Add the salt pork and cover the beans with cold water. Place the beans on the stove over medium heat and bring the beans to a boil. Once the beans are at a rolling boil, reduce the heat to low. Place a lid on the pot and simmer the beans about 45 minutes. Stir the beans occasionally during the entire cooking process. Add water if needed to keep the beans covered in water.

Stir in the onion, parsley, green bell pepper, garlic, salt, cayenne pepper, black pepper, Tabasco sauce, Worcestershire sauce, tomato sauce, oregano and thyme. Simmer about 1 hour. Stir in the sausage and simmer for 45 minutes. The beans should be tender and the sausage done when ready. Remove the pot from the heat. Place the rice in serving bowls. Spoon the beans, sausage and bean liquid over the rice and serve.

Sweet Sour Red Beans

Makes 12 servings

2 lbs. dry kidney beans
Water
3 tsp. salt
1/2 cup light brown sugar
1/2 cup cider vinegar
1 cup green onions, chopped

In a large pot, add the beans. Cover the beans with cold water about 2" above the beans. Place a lid on the pot and let the beans soak for 24 hours. Pour the water off the beans and rinse the beans with fresh cold water.

Add cold water to the beans to about 2" above the beans. Place the beans on the stove over medium heat. Bring the beans to a rolling boil and reduce the heat to medium low. Simmer the beans for 1 1/2 to 2 hours or until the beans are tender. If the water is evaporating from the beans, add additional water as needed to keep the beans covered in water.

When the beans are tender, add the salt, brown sugar and cider vinegar. Stir until well combined. Simmer the beans for 15 minutes to combine the flavors. Remove the pot from the heat and sprinkle the green onions over the top of the beans before serving.

Red Beans and Rice

Makes 8 servings

1 lb. salt pork
Water
1 lb. red kidney beans
2 garlic cloves, chopped
1 tsp. Italian seasoning
1 green bell pepper, diced
1 onion, chopped
1/4 cup celery, chopped
1 jalapeno pepper, diced
Salt to taste
4 cups hot cooked rice

In a large pot, add the salt pork. Cover the salt pork with water. Place the pot on the stove over medium heat. Bring the salt pork to a boil and boil for 5 minutes. Remove the pot from the stove and drain off all the water. Rinse the salt pork with cold water.

Dice the salt pork and place back in the pot. Add the kidney beans, garlic, Italian seasoning, green bell pepper, onion, celery and jalapeno pepper. Add cold water to about 3" above the beans and vegetables. Place the pot back on the stove over medium heat. Bring the beans to a boil and reduce the heat to low.

Simmer the beans and pork for 2-3 hours or until the beans are tender and the bean liquid thickens. Remove the pan from the heat and season with salt to taste. Serve over hot cooked rice.

Smoked Sausage Red Beans & Rice

Makes 10 servings

1 lb. dried red beans
2 large onions, chopped
2 stalks celery, chopped
1 green bell pepper, chopped
1 garlic clove, minced
Water
2 tsp. salt
1/2 tsp. black pepper
1/4 cup fresh minced parsley
2 lbs. fully cooked smoked sausage
5 cups hot cooked rice

Wash the red beans and remove any bad beans. Place the beans, onions, celery, green bell pepper and garlic in a dutch oven. Cover the beans with water and place the beans on the stove over medium heat. Bring the beans to a boil and reduce the heat to low. Place a lid on the beans. Simmer the beans for 2 to 2 1/2 hours or until the beans are tender. Add additional water to the beans if needed to keep the beans covered with water. A thick gravy like broth should have formed on the beans.

Stir in the salt, black pepper and parsley. Cook for 5 minutes. Remove the pan from the heat and keep the beans warm. Slice the smoked sausage into 1/4" slices. Add the smoked sausage to a skillet over medium heat. Brown the sausage about 8 minutes. The sausage slices should be hot and well browned. Remove the skillet from the heat.

Spoon the rice onto a large serving platter. Place the sausage slices over the rice. Spoon the beans and gravy around the rice on the platter and serve.

Slow Cooker New Orleans Red Beans & Rice

Makes 10 servings

1 lb. dried red beans
Water
1 green bell pepper, chopped
1 onion, chopped
3 celery stalks, chopped
3 garlic cloves, chopped
8 oz. Andouille sausage, chopped
3 tbs. Creole seasoning
5 cups hot cooked rice
1/2 cup sliced green onions

Add the dried red beans to a large pot over medium high heat. Cover the beans with cold water and bring the beans to a boil. Boil for 1 minute. Remove the pot from the heat and place a lid on the beans. Let the beans rest for 10 minutes. Drain all the water from the beans. Rinse the beans with cold water.

Add the beans, 7 cups water, green bell pepper, onion, celery stalks, garlic, Andouille sausage and Creole seasoning to the slow cooker. Stir until combined. Cook on low temperature for 5-7 hours or until the beans are tender. When ready to serve, place 1/2 cup rice in each serving bowl. Spoon the beans and sauce over the rice. Garnish each serving with green onions.

Red Beans & Couscous

Makes 8 servings

1 3/4 cups chicken broth
14 oz. can diced tomatoes
1 tsp. salt
1/2 tsp. dried crushed red pepper flakes
1/2 tsp. dried basil
1/2 tsp. dried oregano
10 oz. pkg. quick cooking couscous
15 oz. can red kidney beans, rinsed and drained
2 tbs. olive oil
4 green onions, diced
1/2 cup diced green bell pepper
1/4 cup chopped fresh parsley
1 celery rib, diced
2 garlic cloves, minced
Salt and black pepper to taste

In a large sauce pan over medium high heat, add the chicken broth, tomatoes with juice, salt, red pepper flakes, basil and oregano. Stir until combined and bring the liquids to a boil. When the liquids are boiling, stir in the couscous. Remove the pan from the heat and place a lid on the pan. Let the couscous sit undisturbed for 10 minutes.

When the couscous is ready, fluff the couscous with a fork. Stir in the kidney beans, olive oil, green onions, green bell pepper, parsley, celery and garlic. Stir until well combined.

You can serve the dish at room temperature or place the pan back on the stove for a few minutes to heat the beans and vegetables if desired. Season to taste with salt and black pepper.

Spinach Bean Lasagna

Makes 8 servings

4 cups cooked kidney beans
1 3/4 cups water
28 oz. jar spaghetti sauce
10 oz. pkg. frozen spinach, thawed and well drained
15 oz. container ricotta cheese
2 eggs
10 lasagna noodles, uncooked
1 cup shredded mozzarella cheese
1/4 cup grated Parmesan cheese

Add the beans and water to the food processor. Process until the beans are chopped. Add the beans and spaghetti sauce to a sauce pan over medium high heat. Bring the sauce to a boil and reduce the heat to low. Stir occasionally and simmer for 10 minutes. Remove the pan from the heat.

In a separate bowl, stir together the spinach, ricotta cheese and eggs. Spray a 9 x 13 baking dish with non stick cooking spray. Spread a thin layer of the bean and spaghetti sauce over the bottom of the casserole dish. Layer 5 noodles in the bottom of the dish. Spread half of the spinach mixture over the noodles. Sprinkle half of the mozzarella cheese over the spinach mixture. Spoon half of the sauce over the cheese.

Repeat the layering process one more time using the remaining noodles, spinach mixture, mozzarella cheese and sauce. Cover the dish with aluminum foil and refrigerate the lasagna for 24 hours. Remove the lasagna from the refrigerator. Let the lasagna sit at room temperature for 30 minutes.

Preheat the oven to 350°. Bake the lasagna for 1 hour or until the lasagna is hot and bubbly. Remove the aluminum foil and sprinkle the Parmesan cheese over the top. Bake for 15 minutes. Remove the lasagna from the oven and cool for 10 minutes before serving.

Texas Sausage, Beans & Rice

Makes 8 servings

1 lb. dried kidney beans
Water
1 ham bone
2 large onions, chopped
1 green bell pepper, chopped
2 stalks celery, chopped
3 garlic cloves, chopped
1 bay leaf
1/2 tsp. salt
1/4 tsp. black pepper
1 lb. hot ground pork sausage
1 lb. mild ground pork sausage
1/4 cup minced fresh parsley
4 cups hot cooked rice

In a large pot, add the kidney beans. Add cold water to cover the beans about 2" above the beans. Place a lid on the pot and let the beans soak for 24 hours. Pour the water off the beans and rinse the beans with fresh cold water.

Add fresh water to the beans until they are covered in water about 2" above the beans. Place the beans on the stove over medium heat. Bring the beans to a rolling boil and reduce the heat to medium low. Add the ham bone, onions, green bell pepper, celery, garlic, bay leaf, salt and black pepper to the beans. Stir until combined and place a lid on the pot. Simmer the beans about 1 1/2 to 2 hours or until the beans are tender.

While the beans are cooking, add the hot and mild pork sausage to a skillet over medium heat. Stir frequently to break the meat into crumbles as it cooks. Cook about 10-12 minutes or until the sausage is browned and no longer pink. Remove the skillet from the heat and drain off the excess grease.

Stir the sausage into the beans when the beans are done. Cook for 15 minutes. Remove the ham bone and bay leaf. Discard the bay leaf. Remove the meat from the ham bone and add the ham back to the pot if desired. Remove the pot from the heat. Spoon the rice into bowls and spoon the beans, sausage and juice over the rice.

Bean and Cornbread Casserole

Makes 8 servings

4 tbs. vegetable oil
1 cup chopped onion
1/2 cup chopped green bell pepper
2 garlic cloves, minced
16 oz. can kidney beans, drained
16 oz. can pinto beans, drained
16 oz. can diced tomatoes
1 cup tomato sauce
1 tsp. chili powder
1/2 tsp. black pepper
1/2 tsp. yellow prepared mustard
1/8 tsp. Tabasco sauce
1 cup plain yellow cornmeal
1 cup all purpose flour
2 1/2 tsp. baking powder
1/2 tsp. salt
1 tbs. granulated sugar
3 eggs
1 1/4 cups whole milk
1 cup cream style corn

In a large skillet over medium high heat, add 1 tablespoon vegetable oil. When the oil is hot and shimmers, add the onion, green bell pepper and garlic. Stir constantly and saute the vegetables for 4 minutes. Stir in the kidney beans, pinto beans, tomatoes with juice, tomato sauce, chili powder, black pepper, mustard and Tabasco sauce. Stir until well combined and simmer for 5 minutes. Remove the skillet from the heat.

Preheat the oven to 375°. Spray a 9 x 13 baking dish with non stick cooking spray. Spoon the bean mixture from the skillet into the baking dish. In a mixing bowl, add the cornmeal, all purpose flour, baking powder, salt and granulated sugar. Whisk until well combined. In a separate bowl, stir together the eggs, whole milk, 3 tablespoons vegetable oil and corn. Whisk until well combined and add to the dry ingredients. Mix only until the batter is combined. Spoon the batter over the beans in the casserole dish. Bake for 30-35 minutes or until the cornbread is done and golden brown.

Remove the casserole from the oven and serve. Garnish with green bell pepper strips and green onions if desired.

Spicy Mexican Bean Casserole

Makes 8 servings

1 cup sour cream
1 cup cream style cottage cheese
2 cups shredded Monterey Jack cheese
1/4 cup chopped green onion
2 tbs. diced green chiles
1/4 tsp. salt
2 tbs. chopped green bell pepper
1 garlic clove, minced
1 tbs. vegetable oil
16 oz. can diced tomatoes
4 cups cooked red kidney beans
1 cup tomato sauce
1 1/2 tsp. chili powder
1/2 cup sliced black olives
2 cups crushed corn chips
1 cup shredded sharp cheddar cheese

In a mixing bowl, add the sour cream, cottage cheese, Monterey Jack cheese, green onion, green chiles and salt. Stir until well combined. Set the bowl aside for the moment.

In a skillet over medium heat, add the green bell pepper, garlic and vegetable oil. Saute the vegetables for 4 minutes. Stir in the tomatoes with juice, kidney beans, tomato sauce, chili powder and black olives. Stir frequently and simmer for 5 minutes. Remove the skillet from the heat.

Preheat the oven to 350°. Spray a 2 1/2 quart casserole dish with non stick cooking spray. Sprinkle 1/2 cup corn chips in the bottom of the casserole dish. Spoon half of the sour cream mixture over the corn chips. Top the sour cream mixture with half of the bean mixture. Sprinkle 3/4 cup corn chips over the top of the bean mixture. Spread the remaining sour cream mixture over the top of the corn chips. Spoon the remaining bean mixture over the sour cream.

Bake for 30 minutes or until the dish is hot and bubbly. Sprinkle the remaining corn chips over the top of the casserole. Sprinkle the cheddar cheese over the top of the casserole. Bake for 5-10 minutes or until the cheese is melted and bubbly. Remove the dish from the oven and serve.

Kidney Bean Salsa

Makes 2 1/2 cups

16 oz. can dark red kidney beans, rinsed and drained
2 serrano chile peppers, seeded and chopped
2 green onions, chopped
1/2 cup chopped purple onion
2 garlic cloves, pressed
2 tbs. fresh chopped cilantro
1/4 cup orange juice
2 tbs. lemon juice
2 tbs. olive oil
1 tbs. red wine vinegar

Add all the ingredients to a mixing bowl. Toss until combined. Cover the bowl and chill at least 2 hours before serving. Serve with savory pancakes, tacos, fajitas or chips.

Ham Bone Red Beans & Rice

Makes 8 servings

1 lb. dried red beans
Water
1 meaty ham bone
3 cups chopped onion
1 cup chopped celery
1 cup minced fresh parsley
3 garlic cloves, minced
1 tbs. salt
1/8 tsp. Tabasco sauce
1 tsp. black pepper
1/4 tsp. dried oregano
1/4 tsp. dried thyme
1 tbs. Worcestershire sauce
1/2 cup tomato sauce
4 cups hot cooked rice

Place the beans in a large pot. Cover the beans with cold water about 3" above the beans. Let the beans soak at least 8 hours but no longer than 36 hours. Drain the beans after soaking and rinse with cold water.

Add the beans and ham bone to a large pot. Cover the beans and ham bone with cold water. Place the pot over medium heat and bring the beans to a boil. When the beans are boiling, reduce the heat to low. Simmer the beans for 2 hours.

You may need to add water as the beans cook. Keep the beans and ham bone covered in water. Stir in the onion, celery, parsley, garlic, salt, Tabasco sauce, black pepper, oregano, thyme, Worcestershire sauce and tomato sauce. Simmer the beans for 1 to 1 1/2 hours or until the beans are tender. Remove the beans from the heat.

Remove the ham bone from the pot. Remove any ham from the bone and add back to the pot. Place the rice in 8 serving bowls. Spoon the beans and broth over the rice. Serve with crusty rolls or cornbread to soak up the juice.

4 LENTILS

Besides being nutritious, lentils are quick and easy to prepare. In less than hour, you can have a pot of lentils ready for recipes. We love lentil tacos. This is my family's favorite bean taco dish. Lentils come in several color varieties. Use whatever variety you have on hand for the recipes.

Lentil Burritos

Makes 8 servings

1 cup dried lentils
4 cups water
1 onion, chopped
1 green bell pepper, chopped
1 tbs. vegetable oil
1 cup shredded cheddar cheese
16 flour tortillas, 7" size
8 oz. can tomato sauce with garlic
1 tsp. ground cumin
1 tbs. taco sauce
1 tsp. cornstarch
Sour cream & guacamole, optional

In a large sauce pan over medium heat, add the lentils and water. Bring the lentils to a boil. Place a lid on the pan and simmer the lentils for 20 minutes or until the lentils are tender. Remove the pan from the heat. Drain the lentils but reserve 1 cup lentil liquid.

In a large skillet over medium heat, add the onion, green bell pepper and vegetable oil. Saute the onion and green pepper for 5 minutes. Stir in the lentils and cheddar cheese. Remove the skillet from the heat.

Preheat the oven to 350°. Spray a 9 x 13 baking dish with non stick cooking spray. Spoon the lentil mixture down the center of each tortilla. Roll the tortillas up and place, seam side down, in the baking dish.

In a sauce pan over medium heat, add 3/4 cup bean liquid, tomato sauce, cumin and taco sauce. Stir constantly and bring the liquids to a boil. In a small bowl, stir together 1/4 cup bean liquid and the cornstarch. Slowly stir the cornstarch mixture into the sauce pan. Stir frequently and simmer about 10 minutes. Pour the sauce over the burritos. Place the baking dish in the oven and bake for 10 minutes or until the burritos are thoroughly heated. Remove the burritos from the oven and top with sour cream and guacamole if desired.

Tomato Baked Lentils

Makes 6 servings

1 cup dried lentils
4 cups water
2 cups cooked whole kernel corn
29 oz. can diced tomatoes
1 tsp. granulated sugar
1/8 tsp. black pepper
1 tsp. seasoned salt
1 cup buttered soft bread crumbs
1/2 cup shredded cheddar cheese
1/8 tsp. paprika

Place the lentils in a large sauce pan with 4 cups water. Place the pan over medium heat and bring the lentils to a boil. Boil the lentils for 2 minutes. Remove the lentils from the heat. Place a lid on the pot and let the lentils sit for 1 hour.

Place the lentils back on the stove over medium heat. Simmer the lentils for 30-45 minutes or until the lentils are tender. Remove the lentils from the heat and drain all the water from the lentils.

Preheat the oven to 375°. Place the corn in the bottom of a 2 quart shallow baking dish. Spoon the lentils over the corn. In a mixing bowl, stir together the tomatoes with juice, granulated sugar, black pepper and season salt. Spoon the mixture over the lentils. Sprinkle the bread crumbs over the top of the casserole. Sprinkle the cheddar cheese and paprika over the top. Bake for 30 minutes or until the casserole is hot and bubbly. Remove the casserole from the oven and serve.

Cheesy Pasta and Lentils

Makes 6 servings

1 1/2 cups dried lentils
1 onion, chopped
3 1/2 cups water
1/2 tsp. salt
1/4 tsp. black pepper
29 oz. jar chunky garlic and herb spaghetti sauce
2 carrots, thinly sliced
2 celery ribs, sliced
1 green bell pepper, chopped
8 oz. rotini pasta, cooked
2 tbs. chopped fresh parsley
1 cup shredded cheddar cheese

In a dutch oven over medium heat, add the lentils, onion, water, salt and black pepper. Bring the lentils to a boil and place a lid on the pan. Simmer the lentils for 35 minutes. Stir in the spaghetti sauce, carrots, celery and green bell pepper. Simmer about 20 minutes or until the lentils and vegetables are tender.

Stir in the pasta and parsley. Cook only until the pasta is heated. Remove the pot from the heat and sprinkle the cheddar cheese over the top.

Lentil Tacos

Makes 4 servings

1 1/2 cups dried lentils
3 to 5 cups water
1 bay leaf
1 stalk celery
1 garlic clove, crushed
1/2 tsp. salt
1/8 tsp. dried thyme
1 1/2 cups tomato sauce
1 tbs. taco seasoning mix
8 hot taco shells
1 1/2 cups shredded lettuce
1 onion, diced
1 cup shredded cheddar cheese
1 tomato, chopped

Rinse the lentils with cold water and remove any bad lentils. Add the lentils, 3 1/2 cups water, bay leaf, celery stalk, garlic, salt and thyme to a large sauce pan. Place the pan over medium heat and bring the lentils to a boil. When the lentils are boiling, reduce the heat to low and place a lid on the pan. Simmer the lentils about 1 1/2 hours or until the lentils are tender.

Stir the lentils occasionally and add the remaining water if needed to keep the lentils covered with water while cooking. Remove the celery stalk and bay leaf from the lentils and discard. Remove the pan from the heat and drain off the excess water from the lentils.

In a small bowl, stir together the tomato sauce and taco seasoning mix. Spoon the lentils into the taco shells and drizzle the tomato taco sauce over the lentils. Sprinkle the lettuce, onion, cheddar cheese and tomato over each taco before serving.

Lentil Samosas

Makes 3 dozen

1/2 cup dried lentils
2 garlic cloves, minced
2 carrots, peeled and diced
1 onion, diced
1/2 tsp. salt
1 tsp. cayenne pepper
1 tsp. curry powder
2 tbs. chopped fresh cilantro
9 egg roll wrappers
Vegetable oil for frying
Mango chutney, optional

In a large sauce pan over medium heat, add the lentils, garlic, carrots, onion, salt, cayenne pepper and curry powder. Cover the lentils with cold water and bring the lentils to a boil. When the lentils are at a full boil, reduce the heat to low and place a lid on the sauce pan. Simmer the lentils about 25 minutes or until the lentils are tender. Remove the pan from the heat and drain off any liquid. Stir in the cilantro.

Cut each egg roll wrapper into 4 squares. Spoon 1 teaspoon of the lentil mixture on one half of the wrapper. Moisten the wrapper edges with water. Fold the wrapper over the filling. Using the tines of a fork, seal the edges.

In a skillet over medium high heat, add vegetable oil to a 1" depth in the skillet. The oil needs to be about 375° when ready. Reduce the heat or increase the heat on your stove if needed to maintain the frying temperature. Medium high heat works on my stove. When the oil is hot, add a few wrappers to the skillet. I only do three or four at a time. The oil temperature will drop too fast if you overcrowd the skillet.

Fry about 15 seconds on each side. Remove the wrappers from the skillet and drain on paper towels. Fry the remaining wrappers. Place the wrappers on a serving platter. Serve hot with mango chutney if desired.

Lentil Burgers

Makes 8 servings

1 cup dried lentils
2 1/2 cups water
1/4 cup ketchup
1/4 tsp. garlic powder
1 onion, chopped
1 cup uncooked quick cooking oats
1 egg
1/2 tsp. salt
1 tbs. whole wheat flour
2 tbs. vegetable oil

In a sauce pan over medium heat, add the lentils and water. Bring the lentils to a boil. When the lentils are boiling, place a lid on the pan and reduce the heat to low. Simmer the lentils for 30 minutes. Remove the lid on the pan and simmer the lentils for 10 minutes. Most of the liquid should be absorbed and the lentils tender when ready. Stir in the ketchup, garlic powder, onion, oats, egg and salt. Stir until well combined. Remove the pan from the heat.

Form the lentil mixture into 8 patties. Sprinkle the whole wheat flour over the patties. Place the patties on a baking sheet. Cover the baking sheet and chill for 1 hour.

When the patties are chilled, add 1 tablespoon vegetable oil to a skillet. Place 4 patties in the skillet. Cook about 2 minutes per side. The patties should be browned and hot when ready. Remove the patties from the skillet and keep warm. Repeat the step adding the remaining vegetable oil and patties to the skillet. When all the patties are cooked, serve on hamburger buns with your favorite fixings if desired.

Lentil and Rice Supper

Makes 8 servings

6 cups water
1 3/4 cup dried lentils
1/2 tsp. ground turmeric
1 tbs. dried coriander
2 medium yellow squash, sliced
8 oz. fresh mushrooms, sliced
1 green bell pepper, chopped
1 onion, chopped
1 tbs. Worcestershire sauce
2 tsp. salt
1 tbs. vegetable oil
1/2 tsp. cumin seeds
1/4 tsp. coarse ground black pepper
1/2 tsp. Tabasco sauce
4 cups hot cooked rice

In a large sauce pan over medium heat, add the water, lentils, turmeric and coriander. Stir until combined and bring the lentils to a boil. Place a lid on the pan and reduce the heat to low. Simmer the lentils about 1 hour or until they are tender.

Stir in the squash, mushrooms, green bell pepper, onion, Worcestershire sauce and salt. Stir occasionally and simmer about 20 minutes or until the vegetables are tender.

While the vegetables are cooking, add the cumin seeds and black pepper to a small skillet over medium heat. Stir constantly and cook for 1 minute. The cumin seeds should be toasted. Remove the skillet from the heat and add to the lentils. Stir in the Tabasco sauce and remove the lentils from the heat.

Place the rice on a serving platter. Spoon the lentils and any liquid over the rice and serve.

Lentil Rice Casserole

Makes 5 servings

1 tsp. unsalted butter, softened
1 cup chopped onion
2 garlic cloves, minced
1 cup chopped green bell pepper
1 cup dried lentils, cooked
14 oz. can diced tomatoes
1 tsp. paprika
1/4 tsp. salt
1/2 tsp. black pepper
1/2 tsp. cayenne pepper
2 cups cooked brown rice
1 1/2 cups shredded cheddar cheese

In a large skillet over medium heat, add the butter, onion, garlic and green bell pepper. Saute the vegetables for 5 minutes. Stir in the cooked lentils, tomatoes with juice, paprika, salt, black pepper and cayenne pepper. Stir until well combined. Reduce the heat to low and place a lid on the skillet. Simmer for 20 minutes. Remove the pan from the heat.

Preheat the oven to 325°. Spray a 2 quart casserole dish with non stick cooking spray. Spread the rice in the bottom of the casserole dish. Pour the lentil mixture over the rice. Bake for 15 minutes. Sprinkle the cheddar cheese over the top of the casserole. Bake for 5-8 minutes or until the casserole is hot, bubbly and the cheese melted. Remove the casserole from the oven and serve.

Tex Mex Lentils

Makes 8 servings

3 1/2 cups dried lentils
7 cups water
16 oz. can Mexican style diced tomatoes
12 oz. can tomato paste
1/2 cup bulgur wheat
2 tbs. chili powder
2 tsp. salt
1/2 tsp. black pepper
1/2 tsp. dried thyme
3 garlic cloves, minced
1 onion, chopped
1 tbs. red wine vinegar
Shredded cheese, optional (use your favorite flavor)

In a dutch oven over medium heat, add the lentils and water. Bring the lentils to a boil. Place a lid on the pot and simmer the lentils about 40 minutes. If the water is evaporating too quickly, reduce the heat to low.

Stir in the tomatoes with juice, tomato paste, bulgur wheat, chili powder, salt, black pepper, thyme, garlic and onion. Stir until well combined and bring the lentils to a boil. When the lentils are boiling, reduce the heat to low. Place the lid back on the pan and simmer about 1 hour. Stir occasionally and cook until the lentils are tender. Remove the pan from the heat and stir in the red wine vinegar.

Sprinkle shredded cheese over the top of each serving if desired.

Baked Lentils with Cheese

Makes 6 servings

1 1/2 cups lentils
2 cups tomato sauce
2 cups water
1 onion, chopped
2 garlic cloves, minced
1 1/2 tsp. salt
2 bay leaves
1/4 tsp. black pepper
1/4 tsp. ground sage
3/4 tsp. dried marjoram
2 carrots, thinly sliced
1 cup celery, thinly sliced
1 green bell pepper, chopped
2 tbs. minced fresh parsley
1 1/2 cups shredded cheddar cheese

Spray a 3 quart casserole dish with non stick cooking spray. Preheat the oven to 375°. Add the lentils, tomato sauce, water, onion, garlic, salt, bay leaves, black pepper, sage, marjoram and carrots to the casserole dish. Stir until well combined. Cover the casserole dish with a lid or aluminum foil. Bake for 30 minutes.

Stir the celery and green bell pepper into the casserole dish. Cover the dish and bake for 30 minutes or until the vegetables and lentils are tender. Take the cover off the dish and sprinkle the parsley and cheddar cheese over the top of the casserole. Bake for 5-10 minutes or until the cheese is melted and bubbly. Remove the dish from the oven and serve.

Bean Pot Lentils

Makes 4 servings

5 cups chicken broth
1 cup dried lentils
1/2 cup chopped onion
2 tbs. light brown sugar
2 tbs. ketchup
2 tbs. molasses
1 tbs. yellow prepared mustard
2 slices bacon, cooked and diced

In a large sauce pan over medium heat, add the chicken broth, lentils and onion. Bring the lentils to a boil. When the lentils are boiling, place a lid on the pan and simmer the lentils about 45 minutes or until the lentils are tender.

Stir in the brown sugar, ketchup, molasses and mustard and remove the pan from the heat. Preheat the oven to 325°. Spray a 1 1/2 quart casserole dish with non stick cooking spray. Spoon the lentils into the casserole dish. Sprinkle the bacon over the top. Bake for 1 hour. The lentils should be creamy and most of the liquid absorbed when ready. Remove the dish from the oven and serve.

Lentil Pate

Makes about 2 cups

3/4 cup dried lentils
3 cups water
2 hard boiled eggs
1 1/2 cups chopped onion
1 tbs. vegetable oil
2 garlic cloves, minced
1/2 tsp. salt
1/4 tsp. black pepper
1/8 tsp. ground nutmeg
1/4 tsp. hot sauce
1/8 tsp. liquid smoke

In a sauce pan over medium heat, add the lentils and water. Bring the lentils to a boil. When the lentils are at a rolling boil, place a lid on the pan. Reduce the heat to low and simmer the lentils about 35 minutes or until the lentils are tender. Remove the pan from the heat and drain off the liquid. Set the lentils aside for the moment.

Peel the eggs if you have not already done this step. Remove the yolks and discard. In a skillet over medium heat, add the onion and vegetable oil. Stir constantly and saute the onion about 4 minutes or until the onion is tender. Remove the skillet from the heat.

To a food processor bowl, add the lentils, egg whites, onion, garlic, salt, black pepper, nutmeg, hot sauce and liquid smoke. Process until smooth or about 2 minutes. Spoon the pate into a serving bowl. Cover the bowl and refrigerate until well chilled. Serve with crackers or vegetables.

Lentil Spread

Makes 3/4 cup

1/4 cup dried lentils
3/4 cup water or chicken broth
1 tbs. lemon juice
1 tsp. sesame oil
1/4 tsp. salt
1/4 tsp. cayenne pepper
2 garlic cloves, minced

In a sauce pan over medium heat, add the lentils and water. Bring the lentils to a boil and place a lid on the pan. Simmer the lentils about 25 minutes or until the lentils are tender. Remove the pan from the heat and drain off the liquid.

Add the lentils, lemon juice, sesame oil, salt, cayenne pepper and garlic to a food processor. Process until smooth. Scrape down the sides of the bowl if needed. Spoon the spread into a serving bowl. Cover the bowl and chill if desired. The spread will keep for 3 days in the refrigerator. Serve with crackers or fresh veggies.

5 BLACK BEANS

Black beans take longer to cook but they are delicious in ethnic dishes. They make the best bean enchiladas. I cook dried black beans in the slow cooker. I soak the beans overnight and cook them with onion and garlic. The bean liquid from black beans will be dark. I rinse the beans before using in recipes.

You can substitute canned black beans in the recipes if desired. Rinse and drain black beans before using in any recipe.

Black Bean & Rice Tostados

Makes 4 servings

4 corn tortillas, 6" size
15 oz. can black beans, rinsed and drained
1/4 cup vegetable broth
2 tbs. chopped green chiles
1/2 tsp. ground cumin
1/2 tsp. garlic powder
1/4 tsp. salt
2 cups hot cooked rice
Cheese, lettuce, tomato, onion, salsa & guacamole as desired

Preheat the oven to 350°. Place the corn tortillas on a baking sheet. Bake for 5 minutes or until both sides of the tortillas are crisp. Remove the tortillas from the oven and keep warm.

In a large sauce pan over medium heat, add the black beans, vegetable broth, green chiles, cumin, garlic powder, salt and rice. Stir constantly and cook until the mixture comes to a boil. Remove the pan from the heat and drain off all liquid.

Spoon the black bean mixture over the crispy tostadas. Top with cheese, lettuce, tomato, onion, salsa and guacamole if desired.

Meatless Enchiladas

Makes 6 servings

1 onion, chopped
3 garlic cloves, minced
2 tbs. olive oil
16 oz. can diced tomatoes
15 oz. can tomato sauce
1 1/2 tbs. chili powder
1/2 tsp. dried oregano
1/2 tsp. ground cumin
15 oz. can black beans, drained
1 1/2 cups cooked whole kernel corn
1/2 cup sliced black olives
1 cup cottage cheese
2 cups shredded cheddar cheese
4 oz. can diced green chiles, drained
10 corn tortillas, 6" size
1/4 cup olive oil

In a skillet over medium heat, add the onion, garlic and olive oil. Saute the onion and garlic for 4 minutes. Stir in the tomatoes with juice, tomato sauce, chili powder, oregano and cumin. Bring the sauce to a boil. When the sauce is boiling, reduce the heat to low. Simmer the sauce for 20 minutes or until the sauce thickens. Remove the skillet from the heat.

Preheat the oven to 350°. Spray a 9 x 13 baking dish with non stick cooking spray. Spread 1 cup sauce over the bottom of the baking dish. Add the black beans, corn and black olives to the remaining sauce in the skillet. In a mixing bowl, add the cottage cheese, 3/4 cup cheddar cheese and green chiles. Stir until combined. Set the bowl aside for the moment.

In a skillet over medium heat, add the olive oil. When the olive oil is hot, fry each tortilla in the oil. Only fry for a few seconds or until the tortilla is soft. You have to roll the tortilla and you only need to fry to soften the tortillas. Spoon about 2 tablespoons of the cottage cheese mixture in the center of each tortilla. Roll the tortilla up and place, seam side down, in the baking dish. Spoon the remaining sauce over the tortillas.

Cover the dish with aluminum foil. Bake for 20 minutes. Remove the aluminum foil and sprinkle the remaining 1 1/4 cups cheddar cheese over the top. Bake for 8-10 minutes or until the enchiladas are hot, bubbly and the cheese melted. Remove the dish from the oven and serve.

Spicy Beef and Black Beans

Makes 4 servings

2 cans drained Rotel tomatoes, 10 oz. size
2 cans rinsed and drained black beans, 15 oz. size
1 onion, diced
2 garlic cloves, minced
1 lb. boneless sirloin steak, thinly sliced
2 cups shredded Monterey Jack cheese
2 cups hot cooked rice, optional

Preheat the oven to 350°. Spray a 11 x 7 baking dish with non stick cooking spray. In a mixing bowl, stir together the Rotel tomatoes, black beans, onion and garlic. Place half of the sirloin steak slices in the bottom of the baking dish. Spoon half of the Rotel mixture over the steak. Repeat with another layer of sirloin steak and the remaining Rotel mixture over the steak.

Bake for 30 minutes or until the steak is cooked and the dish hot and bubbly. Sprinkle the Monterey Jack cheese over the top and bake for 5 minutes. Remove the dish from the oven and serve over rice if desired.

Marinated Black Beans

Makes 10 servings

1/3 cup red wine vinegar
1/3 cup olive oil
3/4 tsp. salt
1/2 tsp. black pepper
3 garlic cloves, crushed
6 cups cooked black beans, rinsed and drained
10 oz. pkg. frozen whole kernel corn, thawed
1 red bell pepper, chopped
1 green bell pepper, chopped
1 purple onion, chopped

In a mixing bowl, add the red wine vinegar, olive oil, salt, black pepper and garlic. Stir until combined and let the dressing marinate at room temperature for 30 minutes. In a separate serving bowl, add the black beans, corn, red bell pepper, green bell pepper and purple onion. Pour the dressing over the black beans. Toss until well combined. Cover the bowl and refrigerate at least 8 hours before serving.

Meatless Black Bean Casserole

Makes 6 servings

15 oz. can whole kernel corn, drained
15 oz. can black beans, rinsed and drained
10 oz. can diced tomatoes with green chiles
1 cup sour cream
1 cup picante sauce
2 cups shredded cheddar cheese
2 cups cooked rice
1/4 tsp. black pepper
8 green onions, chopped
1/4 cup sliced black olives
2 cups shredded Monterey Jack cheese

Preheat the oven to 350°. Spray a 9 x 13 baking dish with non stick cooking spray. Add the corn, black beans, tomatoes with green chiles including the liquid, sour cream, picante sauce, cheddar cheese, rice and black pepper. Stir until well combined. Sprinkle the green onions, black olives and Monterey Jack cheese over the top of the casserole.

Bake for 45 minutes or until the casserole is hot and bubbly. Most of the liquid should be absorbed into the rice. Remove the dish from the oven and serve.

Tomato Bean Sauce Pasta Dinner

Makes 6 servings

1 onion, sliced
1 red bell pepper, cut into thin strips
2 garlic cloves, minced
2 tbs. olive oil
8 oz. pkg. sliced fresh mushrooms
29 oz. can diced Italian style tomatoes
15 oz. can black beans, rinsed and drained
15 oz. can kidney beans, rinsed and drained
3 oz. jar capers, drained
1/4 cup sliced black olives
1/4 tsp. salt
1/2 tsp. black pepper
8 oz. angel hair pasta, hot and cooked
1/3 cup crumbled Feta cheese
Salt, cayenne pepper or black pepper to taste

In a large skillet over medium high heat, add the onion, red bell pepper, garlic and olive oil. Saute the vegetables for 3 minutes. Add the mushrooms and saute the mushrooms for 4 minutes. Stir in the tomatoes with juice, black beans, kidney beans, capers, black olives, salt and black pepper. Stir until well combined and bring the sauce to a boil. When the sauce is boiling, reduce the heat to low. Stir occasionally and simmer the sauce about 25 minutes or until the sauce is thickened and combined. Remove the skillet from the heat.

Place the hot pasta on a serving platter. Spoon the sauce over the hot pasta. Sprinkle the Feta cheese over the top. Season to taste with salt, cayenne pepper and black pepper.

Black Bean & Lime Pasta

Makes 3 servings

4 garlic cloves, minced
2 tbs. olive oil
1/3 cup fresh lime juice
1/4 cup dry sherry
1 cup sliced green onions
2 cups diced fresh tomato
15 oz. can black beans, rinsed and drained
2 tsp. grated lime zest
1/2 tsp. salt
1/4 tsp. black pepper
2 1/2 cups small penne or bow tie pasta, hot and cooked
1/4 cup chopped fresh Italian parsley

In a skillet over medium low heat, add the garlic and olive oil. Saute the garlic for 2 minutes. The garlic should be tender but not burnt. Burnt garlic will ruin the dish. Add the fresh lime juice and sherry to the skillet. Increase the heat to medium high and cook until the liquid is reduced to about 1/4 cup.

Reduce the heat to medium and stir in the green onions and tomato. Stir frequently and cook for 5 minutes. Add the black beans, lime zest, salt and black pepper. Stir frequently and cook until the beans are hot. Remove the skillet from the heat.

Place the pasta in a serving bowl. Pour the bean sauce over the pasta and toss until combined. Sprinkle the parsley over the top and serve.

Black Beans with Rice

Makes 8 servings

1 lb. dry black beans
Water
2/3 cup olive oil
6 garlic cloves, minced
2 bay leaves
1 green bell pepper, finely chopped
1/2 cup celery, finely chopped
1 tbs. white vinegar
1/2 tsp. cayenne pepper
1/2 tsp. dried basil
1/2 tsp. dried oregano
Salt and black pepper to taste
4 cups hot cooked rice
1 cup sliced green onions

Place the beans in a large pot. Cover the beans with cold water about 3" above the beans. Let the beans soak for 24 hours. Drain the water from the soaked beans. Rinse the beans with cold water.

In a large sauce pan over medium low heat, add the beans and 1 quart water. Bring the beans to a boil and reduce the heat to low. Simmer the beans for 1 hour. Add the olive oil, garlic, bay leaves, green bell pepper, celery and vinegar. Stir until combined. Simmer the beans for 3-4 hours or until the beans are tender and the bean liquid thickened. Remove the bay leaves and discard.

Ten minutes before the beans are done, add the cayenne pepper, dried basil and oregano to the beans. Stir until combined and season the beans to taste with salt and black pepper. Remove the pan from the heat. Place the rice on a serving platter. Spoon the beans over the rice. Sprinkle the green onions over the beans before serving.

Black Bean Pancakes with Gazpacho Butter

Makes 8 pancakes

1 cup dried black beans
3 cups chicken broth
1 large onion, chopped
1 red bell pepper, chopped
3 jalapeno peppers, seeded and chopped
3 garlic cloves, minced
1 tbs. chopped fresh cilantro
1 tbs. ground cumin
6 tbs. unsalted butter, melted
2 cups port wine
1 1/4 tsp. salt
1/8 tsp. black pepper
1 1/2 cups all purpose flour
1 3/4 tsp. baking powder
3 tbs. granulated sugar
1 egg, beaten
1/2 cup softened unsalted butter
1 tbs. tomato puree
1/2 cup red bell pepper, chopped
1/2 cup yellow bell pepper, chopped
2 tbs. finely chopped cucumber

Rinse the black beans with cold water. Add the beans and chicken broth to a large pot. Place a lid on the pot and soak the beans for 8 hours in the refrigerator. Remove the pot from the refrigerator when the beans are soaked. In a skillet over medium heat, add the onion, 1 chopped red bell pepper, jalapeno peppers, garlic, cilantro, cumin and 3 tablespoons melted butter. Saute the vegetables for 5 minutes. Remove the skillet from the heat and add the vegetables to the beans.

Stir in the port wine, 1/4 teaspoon salt and black pepper to the beans. Place the pot on the stove over medium heat and bring the beans to a boil. When the beans are at a full boil, reduce the heat to low. Place a lid on the pot and simmer the beans for 1 1/2 to 2 hours or until the beans are tender. When the beans are done, remove the beans from the heat. Drain the beans but reserve 1 1/4 cups bean liquid. Add 1 3/4 cups beans to a blender. Process until smooth. Set the bean liquid and puree aside for the moment.

Black Bean Pancakes with Gazpacho Butter cont'd

In a mixing bowl, add the all purpose flour, baking powder, 1 teaspoon salt and granulated sugar. Stir until well combined. Stir in the egg, 3 tablespoons melted butter and bean liquid. Whisk until well combined. Add the reserved bean puree and stir only until combined.

Spray a griddle with non stick cooking spray. Heat the griddle to 350° or medium heat. Spoon 1/4 cup bean batter for each pancake onto the hot griddle. Cook the pancakes about 2 minutes on each side. The edges of the pancake will looked done and slightly crisp when ready. Serve the pancakes with Gazpacho Butter.

To make the Gazpacho Butter, add 1/2 cup softened butter, tomato puree, 1/2 cup red bell pepper, yellow bell pepper and cucumber to a mixing bowl. Stir until well combined.

Black Bean Cakes with Mixed Greens

Makes 4 servings

8 oz. dried black beans
Water
2 eggs
1 cup finely chopped onion
4 oz. smoked Andouille sausage, cut into 1" pieces
6 bacon slices, cooked and crumbled
3/4 tsp. salt
1/2 tsp. Tabasco sauce
2 garlic cloves
1/4 cup whole milk
2 tbs. unsalted butter, melted
3/4 cup all purpose flour
1/2 tsp. black pepper
1 cup apple cider
1/3 cup light brown sugar
1/4 cup toasted finely chopped pecans
3 cups salad greens

Rinse the beans with cold water and remove any bad beans. Add the beans to a large pot. Cover the beans with cold water about 2" above the beans. Place a lid on the pot and soak the beans for 12 hours. Drain all the water from the beans.

Add 2 quarts water to the pot with the beans. Place the pot over medium high heat and bring the beans to a boil. When the beans are at a full boil, reduce the heat to low and place a lid on the pot. Simmer the beans for 1 1/2 to 2 hours or until the beans are tender. Remove the beans from the heat and drain off the liquid. Reserve 1/4 cup bean liquid from the pot.

In the bowl of a food processor, add the beans, 1/4 cup bean liquid, 1 egg, 1/2 cup onion, Andouille sausage, 1 crumbled bacon slice, salt, Tabasco sauce and garlic. Process until the mixture is smooth. In a mixing bowl, add 1 egg, whole milk, melted butter, all purpose flour and black pepper. Whisk until combined and stir in the bean mixture.

Spray a hot skillet or griddle with non stick cooking spray. Spoon 1/4 cup bean batter onto the griddle for each cake. Smooth the batter around to make a 4" cake. When the edges of the bean cakes are cooked, flip them over and cook about 2 minutes on the other side. Remove the bean cakes from the griddle and keep warm.

Black Bean Cakes with Mixed Greens cont'd

To make the dressing for the salad, add 1 cup apple cider, 1/2 cup onion and brown sugar to a sauce pan over medium heat. Bring the dressing to a boil. When the dressing boils, reduce the heat to low Simmer for 5 minutes. Remove the pan from the heat and stir in 5 crumbled bacon slices and the pecans.

To assemble the dinner, place the mixed greens on each serving plate. Spoon the dressing over the greens. Place the bean cakes over the top of the salad and serve.

Black Bean Spaghetti

Makes 6 servings

1 large onion, sliced
1 red bell pepper, cut into thin strips
1 yellow bell pepper, cut into thin strips
8 oz. pkg. sliced fresh mushrooms
2 tbs. olive oil
16 oz. can diced tomatoes
15 oz. can black beans, rinsed and drained
15 oz. can kidney beans
3 1/2 oz. jar capers
1/4 cup sliced black olives
1/4 tsp. dried rosemary
1/4 tsp. dried basil
1/4 tsp. black pepper
4 cups hot cooked angel hair pasta

In a deep skillet over medium heat, add the onion, red bell pepper, yellow bell pepper, mushrooms and olive oil. Saute the vegetables about 5 minutes or until the vegetables are tender. Stir in the tomatoes with juice, black beans, kidney beans with liquid, capers, black olives, rosemary, basil and black pepper.

Bring the sauce to a boil. When the sauce is boiling, reduce the heat to low and simmer the sauce about 30 minutes. Remove the pan from the heat. Spoon the hot angel hair pasta onto a serving platter. Spoon the beans and sauce over the pasta and serve.

Corn Black Bean Cakes with Salmon Salsa

You can make this dish without the salmon salsa but it is just superb with the salsa.

Makes 6 servings

8 oz. pkg. smoked salmon, diced
1/4 cup diced purple onion
3 tbs. chopped fresh cilantro
1 tbs. diced jalapeno pepper
2 tbs. olive oil
1 cup all purpose flour
1 tsp. baking powder
2 eggs
1/4 cup unsalted butter, melted
3/4 cup whole milk
3/4 cup frozen whole kernel corn, thawed
3/4 cup cooked black beans, rinsed and drained
3/4 tsp. salt
3/4 tsp. black pepper
2 tbs. vegetable oil

To make the salsa, add the salmon, purple onion, cilantro, jalapeno pepper and olive oil to a mixing bowl. Stir until well combined. Let the salsa sit at room temperature for 30 minutes.

To make the cakes, add the all purpose flour, baking powder, eggs, melted butter, whole milk, corn, black beans, salt and black pepper to a mixing bowl. Stir until combined. In a skillet over medium heat, add the vegetable oil. When the oil is hot, add the cakes. Use 1/4 cup bean mixture for each cake. Cook about 2-3 minutes per side. The top should be bubbly and the bottom golden brown before you flip each cake. Remove the cakes from the skillet. When ready to serve, place the cakes on a serving platter and spoon the salmon salsa over the cakes.

Cuban Black Beans

Makes 8 servings

1 lb. dried black beans
Water
1 large onion, chopped
1 green bell pepper, chopped
6 garlic cloves, minced
4 oz. jar diced red pimento, drained
1/4 cup olive oil
6 oz. can tomato paste
1 tbs. vinegar
1 tsp. granulated sugar
1 tsp. black pepper
2 tsp. salt
4 cups hot cooked rice
2 cups diced tomatoes
1/2 cup chopped green onions

Rinse the beans with cold water and remove any bad beans. Add the beans to a stock pot. Cover the beans with cold water about 2" above the beans. Place a lid on the pot and soak the beans for 12 hours. When the beans have soaked, drain all the water from the beans. Rinse the beans with cold water and drain again.

In a skillet over medium heat, add the onion, green bell pepper, garlic, red pimento and olive oil. Saute the vegetables for 5 minutes or until the vegetables are tender and lightly browned. Remove the skillet from the heat and the vegetables to the beans. Add 5 cups water, tomato paste, vinegar, granulated sugar and black pepper to the beans. Place the beans on the stove over medium heat and bring the beans to a boil. When the beans are boiling, place a lid on the pot and reduce the heat to low. Simmer the beans for 1 1/2 to 2 hours or until the beans are tender. Remove the beans from the heat and stir the salt into the beans.

Place the rice in serving bowl. Spoon the beans and liquid over the rice. Top the beans with diced tomatoes and green onions and serve.

Spanish Black Beans

Makes 8 servings

1 lb. dried black beans
Water
3 green bell peppers, chopped
2 large onions, chopped
2 garlic cloves, minced
1/2 cup olive oil
1 lb. meaty ham hocks
3 bay leaves
1 1/2 tsp. salt
1/4 cup white wine vinegar

In a large pot, add the beans and enough water to cover about 3" above the beans. Place a lid on the pot and let the beans soak for 24 hours. Pour the water off the beans and rinse the beans with fresh cold water.

In a skillet over medium heat, add the green bell peppers, onions, garlic and olive oil. Saute the vegetables for 5 minutes or until the vegetables are tender. Remove the skillet from the heat and add to the beans. Add 5 cups cold water to the beans in the pot. Place the beans on the stove over medium heat. Bring the beans to a rolling boil and reduce the heat to medium low. Stir in the ham hocks, bay leaves and salt. Bring the beans back to a boil. Simmer the beans for 1 1/2 hours or until the beans are tender. Remove the pan from the heat.

Remove the ham hocks from the beans along with the bay leaf. Discard the bay leaf. Remove the meat from the ham hocks and add the meat back to the beans. Stir in the vinegar and serve over hot cooked rice if desired.

Casserole of Black Beans

Makes 8 servings

1 lb. dried black beans
6 cups water
1 1/2 cups chopped onion
1 1/2 cups chopped celery
1 carrot, chopped
2 garlic cloves, chopped
1 tbs. minced fresh parsley
1 1/2 tbs. salt
1/2 tsp. black pepper
1/4 tsp. dried oregano
2 bay leaves
1/8 tsp. cayenne pepper
1/4 cup unsalted butter
1/4 cup dark rum, optional
Sour cream, optional

In a large pot, add the black beans and water. Bring the beans to a boil and cook for 3 minutes. Remove the pot from the heat and place a lid on the pot. Let the beans sit for 1 hour.

Add the onion, celery, carrot, garlic, parsley, salt, black pepper, oregano, bay leaves and cayenne pepper to the beans. Bring the beans to a boil over medium high heat. When the beans are boiling, reduce the heat to low and place a lid on the pot. Simmer the beans for 2 hours. The beans will not be done at this point. Remove the bay leaves and discard.

Preheat the oven to 350°. Spray a 3 quart casserole dish with non stick cooking spray. Spoon the bean mixture into the casserole dish. Stir in the butter and rum if using the rum. Cover the dish with a lid or aluminum foil. Bake for 1 hour or until the beans are tender and done. Remove the casserole from the oven. Use a slotted spoon and serve the beans and vegetables from the casserole. Top the beans with sour cream if desired.

Black Bean Chili Marsala

Makes 12 cups

1 large onion, chopped
2 garlic cloves, minced
3 tbs. vegetable oil
2 1/2 lb. boneless beef roast, cut into bite size pieces
29 oz. can tomato puree
12 oz. can tomato paste
1 cup Marsala wine
1 cup water
8 oz. can sliced mushrooms, drained
3 tbs. chili powder
2 tsp. season salt
1 tsp. black pepper
2 cans black beans, 15 oz. size
5 cups hot cooked rice

In a large sauce pan over medium heat, add the onion, garlic and vegetable oil. Saute the vegetables for 4 minutes. Add the beef roast, tomato puree, tomato paste, Marsala wine, water, mushrooms, chili powder, season salt and black pepper. Stir until well combined.

Bring the chili to a boil. When the chili is boiling, reduce the heat to low and place a lid on the pan. Simmer for 1 hour. Stir occasionally to combine the ingredients and to keep the chili from sticking to the pan. Stir in the black beans with liquid and simmer for 10 minutes. Taste the chili and add additional chili powder if desired. Remove the pan from the heat. Spoon the rice into serving bowls. Spoon the chili over the rice and serve.

Bean Cassoulet with Cornmeal Dumplings

Makes 6 servings

2 tbs. vegetable oil
2 large onions, chopped
5 garlic cloves, minced
1 poblano chile pepper, seeded and chopped
2 red bell peppers, chopped
3 tbs. chili powder
2 tsp. ground cumin
1 tsp. dried oregano
1 1/4 tsp. salt
28 oz. can diced tomatoes
15 oz. can pinto beans
15 oz. can black beans
1/2 tsp. black pepper
2 cups chopped zucchini
1/2 cup all purpose flour
1/2 cup plain white or yellow cornmeal
1 tsp. baking powder
2 tbs. vegetable shortening
1/4 cup shredded cheddar cheese
2 tbs. minced fresh cilantro, optional
1/2 cup whole milk

In a dutch oven over medium heat, add the vegetable oil, onions and garlic. Stir constantly and saute the onions and garlic about 5 minutes or until the onions are tender. Stir in the poblano pepper and red bell peppers. Stir constantly and cook for 3 minutes. Stir in the chili powder, cumin, oregano and 3/4 teaspoon salt. Stir constantly and cook for 2 minutes.

Stir in the tomatoes with liquid, pinto beans with liquid, black beans with liquid and zucchini. Stir until combined and bring the beans to a boil. When the beans are boiling, reduce the heat to low and simmer about 15 minutes or until the zucchini is tender.

In a mixing bowl, add the all purpose flour, cornmeal, baking powder and 1/2 teaspoon salt. Stir until combined. Add the vegetable shortening to the bowl. Using a pastry blender, cut the shortening into the dry ingredients. The mixture should look like coarse crumbs when the shortening is cut into the dry ingredients. Stir in the cheddar cheese, cilantro and whole milk. Mix only until the batter is moistened and combined.

Bean Cassoulet with Cornmeal Dumplings cont'd

Make sure the beans are boiling before adding the dumplings. If you add dumplings to a cool mixture, the dumplings will be soggy and undercooked. Drop the dumpling batter, by tablespoonfuls, onto the beans. Cook for 5 minutes. Place a lid on the pan and simmer about 10 minutes. Lift the lid on the pan and if the dumplings are not done, cook for 5-7 minutes longer or until the dumplings are done and tender. Keep the lid on the pan when cooking the dumplings.

Remove the pan from the heat and serve immediately. The dumplings should be plump and tender.

Easy Black Beans with Yellow Rice

Makes 4 servings

15 oz. can black beans
3 tbs. fresh lime juice
1 tsp. chili powder
1/2 tsp. ground cumin
2 tbs. minced fresh cilantro
5 oz. pkg. saffron rice mix, prepared

Drain the black beans but reserve 2 tablespoons bean liquid. In a sauce pan over medium heat, add the black beans, reserved bean liquid, lime juice, chili powder and cumin. Sir until well combined. Cook until the beans comes to a boil and are hot. Remove the pan from the heat. Spoon the rice onto a serving platter. Spoon the beans over the rice. Sprinkle the cilantro over the beans before serving.

Vegetarian Burritos

Makes 4 servings

1 tbs. olive oil
1 carrot, peeled and shredded
1 onion, chopped
1 garlic clove, minced
1 cup tomato sauce
10 oz. pkg. frozen chopped broccoli, thawed and drained
10 oz. pkg. frozen whole kernel corn, thawed and drained
2 cups black beans, rinsed and drained
1 tbs. chili powder
1/2 tsp. salt
1/4 tsp. ground cumin
1/8 tsp. Tabasco sauce
8 flour tortillas, 10" size
Salsa, guacamole and cheese, optional

In a large skillet over medium heat, add the olive oil, carrot, onion and garlic. Stir constantly and cook for 2 minutes. Stir in the tomato sauce, broccoli, corn, black beans, chili powder, salt, cumin and Tabasco sauce. Stir until well combined. Place a lid on the skillet and simmer for 5 minutes. Remove the skillet from the heat.

Warm the tortillas in the microwave or in a skillet. Spoon 1/2 cup vegetable mixture down the center of each tortilla. Sprinkle with cheese if desired. Fold the opposite sides of the tortilla over the filling to form a burrito. Serve with salsa and guacamole if desired.

Black Bean Pizza Sauce

Makes 1 1/2 cups

16 oz. can black beans, drained
4 oz. can diced green chiles
1 tsp. instant chicken bouillon granules
1/2 tsp. garlic powder
1/2 tsp. dried cilantro

Add the black beans and green chiles with any liquid to the bowl of a food processor. Process until smooth. Add the chicken bouillon, garlic powder and dried cilantro. Process until smooth.

Use on your favorite pizza crust. Store the unused sauce covered in the refrigerator up to 1 week.

Black Bean Corn Salsa

Makes 4 cups

15 oz. can black beans, rinsed and drained
1 cup frozen corn kernels, thawed
1/2 cup chopped red bell pepper
1/2 cup chopped fresh cilantro
8 green onions, sliced
3 tbs. lime juice
2 tbs. balsamic vinegar
1/2 tsp. ground cumin
1/4 tsp. salt

Add all the ingredients to a large bowl. Toss until well combined. Cover the bowl and refrigerate at least 1 hour. You can refrigerate the salsa up to 3 days if desired.

Black Bean Guacamole

Makes 1 1/3 cups

1/4 cup diced onion
15 oz. can black beans, drained and rinsed
2 tbs. lime juice
2 tbs. orange juice
2 garlic cloves, pressed
1/8 tsp. salt
1/4 tsp. black pepper

Add all the ingredients to a food processor. Pulse until the guacamole is chopped. Scrape down the sides of the food processor to combine all the ingredients. You can leave the guacamole chunky or process until smooth. Serve with crackers, raw veggies or tortilla chips.

Black Bean Dip

Makes 2 cups

2 cups cooked black beans
1 cup tomato sauce
1/2 cup shredded cheddar cheese
1 tsp. chili powder

In a small sauce pan over medium heat, add the black beans and tomato sauce. Stir constantly and bring the black beans to a boil. When the beans are boiling, remove the pan from the heat. Using a potato masher, mash the black beans. When the beans are mashed, stir in the cheddar cheese and chili powder. Remove the pan from the heat and spoon into a serving bowl. Serve the dip warm with toasted pita bread.

6 GREAT NORTHERN & NAVY BEANS

Most people refer to these beans as white beans. They are also called cannellini beans. I cook from dried beans for great northern or navy beans. I soak the beans about 24 hours. They tend to cause more intestinal distress than other beans. The longer soaking time really helps remove some of the gas from the beans. You will actually see little bubbles on top of the soaking water. Be sure to pour off the soaking water and rinse the beans in cold water before using. I use this method for all soaked beans.

There is nothing as delicious as a big pot of white beans with cornbread. The cornbread is great for soaking up all the liquor from the beans. This is the most popular bean for baked beans and pork and beans.

Baked Beans with Ham

Makes 6 servings

1 lb. dried white beans, rinsed and drained
Water
1 onion, sliced
2 tsp. salt
1/4 cup ketchup
1/4 cup molasses
1 tbs. cider vinegar
1/4 tsp. Tabasco sauce
1 tsp. dry mustard
3 lbs. smoked ham shanks

In a large pot, add the beans and 6 cups water. Bring the beans to a boil over medium heat and boil for 2 minutes. Remove the beans from the heat and place a lid on the pot. Let the beans soak for 1 hour.

Place the beans back on the stove over medium heat. Stir in the onion and salt. The beans will absorb the water so add additional water if needed to keep the beans covered while cooking. Cook the beans for 1 to 1 1/2 hours or until the beans are tender but not mushy. They will cook additional time in the oven. Remove the beans from the heat. Drain the beans but reserve the liquid.

Add the bean liquid to a mixing bowl. Stir in the ketchup, molasses, cider vinegar, Tabasco sauce and dry mustard. Preheat the oven to 325°. Place the ham shanks in a 3 quart casserole dish. Pour the beans around the ham. Pour the bean liquid mixture over the beans. Cover the casserole dish with aluminum foil and bake for 1 1/2 hours. Remove the aluminum foil and discard. Remove the ham shanks from the dish. Bake the beans for 1 hour or until the beans are tender and most of the liquid absorbed. Remove the meat from the ham shanks and cut into bite size pieces. Stir the ham into the baked beans. Bake for 30 minutes. Remove the beans from the oven and serve.

Zesty Pork & Beans

Makes 4 servings

4 slices bacon
16 oz. can pork & beans
1/4 cup light brown sugar
2 tsp. dried minced onion
1 tsp. dried oregano
1/4 tsp. garlic salt
1/4 cup ketchup
1/8 tsp. Tabasco sauce

Preheat the oven to 350°. In a skillet over medium heat, add the bacon. Cook for 8 minutes or until the bacon is crispy. Remove the bacon from the skillet and drain on paper towels. Crumble the bacon into pieces.

Save the bacon drippings. Add 2 tablespoons bacon drippings to a 2 quart casserole dish. Add the pork & beans, brown sugar, minced onion, oregano, garlic salt, ketchup, bacon and Tabasco sauce to the casserole dish. Stir until well combined. Bake for 25 minutes or until the dish is hot and bubbly. Remove the dish from the oven and serve.

Can Can Baked Beans

Makes 6 servings

6 cups canned baked beans
1 cup tomato sauce
1 cup chopped onion
1/4 cup light brown sugar
1/2 cup ketchup
2 tbs. yellow prepared mustard
1 tsp. salt
4 drops Tabasco sauce
6 slices cooked Canadian bacon or ham

Preheat the oven to 300°. Spray a 2 quart casserole dish with non stick cooking spray. Add the baked beans, tomato sauce, onion, brown sugar, ketchup, mustard, salt and Tabasco sauce to the casserole dish. Stir until well blended. Add the Canadian bacon slices and toss to cover the bacon slices with the beans. Bake for 2-3 hours or until the beans have browned and most of the liquid is absorbed. Remove the dish from the oven and serve.

To cook in the crock pot, add all the ingredients. Stir until combined. Set the crock pot on low and cook about 6-8 hours. Serve with hot buttered cornbread.

Slow Cooker Bourbon Baked Beans

Makes 12 servings

4 cans Boston baked beans, 16 oz. size
16 oz. can crushed pineapple, drained
12 oz. jar chili sauce
1/2 cup strong brewed coffee
1/2 cup quality bourbon
1/4 cup light brown sugar
1 tbs. molasses
3/4 tsp. dry mustard

Add all the ingredients to a large slow cooker. Stir until well combined. Set the slow cooker to high and cook for 2 hours. Take the lid off the slow cooker and cook until most of the liquid is absorbed. This takes about 1 hour in my slow cooker. Turn the slow cooker off and serve. Use a slotted spoon to remove the beans instead of cooking off the liquid if desired.

Baked Pork & Beans with Ham

Makes 6 servings

1/2 cup finely chopped onion
8 oz. cooked ham, chopped
1 1/2 tbs. vegetable oil
28 oz. can pork and beans
8 oz. can tomato sauce
2 tbs. light brown sugar
1 tbs. Worcestershire sauce
1 tsp. yellow prepared mustard

In a skillet over medium heat, add the onion, ham and vegetable oil. Saute the ham and onion for 5 minutes. The onion should be tender and the ham lightly browned. Remove the pan from the heat.

Preheat the oven to 350°. Spray a 2 quart casserole with non stick cooking spray. Add the ham and onion to the casserole dish. Add the pork and beans with liquid, tomato sauce, brown sugar, Worcestershire sauce and mustard to the casserole dish. Stir until well combined.

Bake for 40 minutes. The beans should be thickened and most of the liquid absorbed when ready. Do not over cook the beans. You still want the beans to be creamy when served. Remove the dish from the oven and serve.

Molasses Baked Beans

Makes 8 servings

2 cans pork and beans, 21 oz. size
1 cup chopped onion
1/2 cup chopped green bell pepper
1/2 cup ketchup
1/3 cup molasses
2 tbs. yellow prepared mustard
2 tsp. chili powder
1/8 tsp. garlic powder
3 slices bacon, cooked crisp and crumbled

Spray a shallow 2 quart casserole dish with non stick cooking spray. Preheat the oven to 350°. Add the pork and beans with liquid, onion, green bell pepper, ketchup, molasses, mustard, chili powder and garlic powder to the casserole dish. Stir until well combined.

Bake for 50-55 minutes or until the beans are hot, bubbly and most of the liquid absorbed when ready. Sprinkle the bacon over the top of the beans before serving. Remove the dish from the oven and serve.

Hawaiian Style Macadamia Baked Beans

Makes 6 servings

2 cans pork and beans, 16 oz. size
8 oz. can pineapple chunks, drained
1/2 cup finely chopped macadamia nuts
1/4 cup chopped green bell pepper
1/4 cup ketchup
3 tbs. light brown sugar
2 tbs. finely chopped onion
1 tbs. soy sauce
1 tbs. vinegar

Preheat the oven to 375°. Spray a 2 quart casserole dish with non stick cooking spray. Add all the ingredients to the casserole dish. Stir until well combined. Bake for 45 minutes or until the dish is hot, bubbly and most of the liquid absorbed when ready. Remove the dish from the oven and serve.

Southern Beef Baked Beans

Makes 6 servings

1 lb. ground beef
1/2 cup chopped onion
28 oz. can pork and beans
1/2 cup ketchup
1 tbs. Worcestershire sauce
1/2 tsp. salt
1/4 tsp. black pepper
1/4 tsp. Tabasco sauce

In a skillet over medium heat, add the ground beef and onion. Stir frequently to break the ground beef into crumbles as it cooks. Cook about 6-7 minutes or until the ground beef is done and no longer pink. Remove the skillet from the heat and drain off the excess grease.

Preheat the oven to 350°. Spoon the ground beef into a 1 1/2 quart casserole dish. Add the pork and beans with liquid, ketchup, Worcestershire sauce, salt, black pepper and Tabasco sauce to the casserole dish. Stir until well combined. Bake for 30 minutes. The beans should be hot, bubbly and most of the liquid absorbed when ready. Remove the dish from the oven and serve.

Easy Hawaiian Baked Beans and Franks

Makes 6 servings

32 oz. can baked beans
1 lb. beef hot dogs, cut into 1" pieces
1 1/2 cups drained crushed pineapple
2 tbs. finely chopped onion
2 tbs. light brown sugar
1 tbs. ketchup
1 tsp. yellow prepared mustard

Preheat the oven to 350°. Add all the ingredients to a 2 quart casserole dish. Stir until well combined. Bake for 45-55 minutes or until the dish is hot, bubbly and most of the liquid absorbed when ready. Remove the dish from the oven and serve.

Three Meat Baked Beans

Makes 4 servings

8 oz. Polish sausage, cut into 1/2" slices
8 oz. ground beef
3 tbs. chopped onion
5 slices bacon, cooked and crumbled
2 cans pork and beans, 16 oz. size
1/3 cup ketchup
1/4 cup light brown sugar
2 tbs. molasses
1 1/2 tsp. Worcestershire sauce
1 1/2 tsp. yellow prepared mustard

In a skillet over medium heat, add the Polish sausage. Cook the sausage until the slices are well browned. Remove the sausage from the skillet and set aside. Add the ground beef and onion to the skillet. Stir frequently to break the meat into crumbles as it cooks. Cook for 6-7 minutes or until the ground beef is well browned and no longer pink. Remove the skillet from the heat and drain off the excess grease.

Preheat the oven to 350°. Spray a 2 quart casserole dish with non stick cooking spray. Add the Polish sausage, ground beef with onion, bacon, pork and beans with liquid, ketchup, brown sugar, molasses, Worcestershire sauce and mustard to the casserole dish. Stir until well combined. Bake for 30 minutes or until the dish is hot, bubbly and most of the liquid absorbed. Remove the dish from the oven and serve.

Skillet Franks & Beans

Makes 6 servings

1 lb. jumbo beef hot dogs, cut into thirds
1/2 cup chopped onion
2 tbs. melted unsalted butter
2 cans pork and beans, 16 oz. size
1/4 cup ketchup
2 tbs. light brown sugar
2 tbs. yellow prepared mustard
1 tbs. Worcestershire sauce

In a large skillet, add the hot dogs, onion and butter. Saute the hot dogs and onion about 5 minutes. The hot dogs and onion should be well browned. Stir in the pork and beans with liquid, ketchup, brown sugar, mustard and Worcestershire sauce. Stir frequently and cook about 12-15 minutes. The dish should be hot, bubbly and most of the liquid evaporated. Remove the skillet from the heat and serve.

Fruited Pork & Beans

Makes 4 servings

16 oz. can pork & beans with liquid
8 oz. can crushed pineapple, drained
1/4 cup light brown sugar
1 tbs. chopped onion
1/4 tsp. ground ginger

Preheat the oven to 350°. Add all the ingredients to a 1 quart casserole dish. Stir until well combined. Bake for 30 minutes or until the beans are hot, bubbly and most of the liquid absorbed. Remove the dish from the oven and serve.

Beefy Baked Beans

Makes 8 servings

1/2 lb. ground beef
31 oz. can pork and beans
1 onion, chopped
1/2 cup green bell pepper, chopped
1/2 cup ketchup
1/2 cup dark corn syrup
2 tbs. yellow prepared mustard
4 slices bacon, cut in half

In a skillet over medium heat, add the ground beef. Stir frequently to break the meat into crumbles as it cooks. Cook about 5 minutes or until the ground beef is well browned and no longer pink. Remove the skillet from the heat and drain off the excess grease.

Preheat the oven to 400°. Spray a 12 x 8 x 2 baking dish with non stick cooking spray. Add the ground beef, pork and beans with liquid, onion, green bell pepper, ketchup, corn syrup and mustard. Stir until well combined.

Arrange the bacon slices on top. Bake for 35-40 minutes. The bacon should be crisp and the beans bubbly when done. Remove the dish from the oven and serve.

Old Fashioned Boston Baked Beans

Makes 8 servings

1 lb. dried navy beans
Water
1/2 cup onion, diced
1/2 cup molasses
1/2 tsp. dry mustard
1/4 cup light brown sugar
1 tsp. salt
1/4 lb. lean salt pork, diced

Place the beans in a large pot. Cover the beans with cold water about 3" above the beans. Soak the beans for 24 hours.

Drain the water from the beans. Place the beans and onion in a large sauce pan over medium heat. Cover the beans with fresh cold water. Bring the beans to a boil and reduce the heat to low. Place a lid on the pan and simmer the beans about 45 minutes. The beans will be ready for the next step when you can easily break the skin on the beans. Remove the pan from the heat. Drain the beans but save the bean liquid.

Preheat the oven to 300°. Spray a 3 quart casserole dish with non stick cooking spray. In a mixing bowl, add the molasses, dry mustard, brown sugar, salt and 1 cup reserved bean liquid. Mix until well combined.

Place half of the salt pork in the casserole dish. Spoon the beans and onion over the pork. Spoon the molasses mixture over the beans. Place the remaining salt pork over the molasses. Press the salt pork down so it comes in contact with the liquids. Cover the dish with aluminum foil and bake for 3-4 hours or until the beans are a deep brown color and most of the liquid is absorbed. Remove the dish from the oven and serve.

Check the beans after 1-2 hours and add additional bean liquid if needed. Some people like their beans dry and some like their beans with more liquid. Add the bean liquid to your taste but do not let the beans get too dry and burn.

Lamb and White Bean Casserole

Makes 4 servings

2 tbs. unsalted butter
1 onion, sliced
1 garlic clove, minced
1/2 tsp. salt
1/2 tsp. dried basil
1/2 tsp. dried rosemary
16 oz. can diced tomatoes, undrained
1 tbs. minced fresh parsley
2 cups cooked lamb, diced
5 cups white beans, cooked
1 bay leaf

In a skillet over medium heat, add the butter. When the butter melts, add the onion and garlic. Saute the onion and garlic for 4 minutes. Add the salt, basil and rosemary. Saute for 1 minute. Add the tomatoes and simmer for 20 minutes. Stir frequently to keep the tomatoes from sticking. Remove the skillet from the heat.

Preheat the oven to 350°. Spoon the tomato mixture into a 2 quart casserole dish. Add the parsley, lamb, white beans and bay leaf. Stir until well combined. Bake for 30 minutes or until the dish is hot and bubbly when ready. Remove the dish from the oven and discard the bay leaf before serving.

Turnip Green White Bean Bake

Makes 4 servings

4 bacon slices
9 cups fresh turnip greens, cleaned and stems removed
1 onion, chopped
3 garlic cloves, minced
1 tbs. minced fresh ginger
1/2 tsp. crushed red pepper flakes
14 oz. can Italian diced tomatoes, drained
15 oz. can great northern beans, drained
1 cup crumbled cornbread
2 tbs. melted unsalted butter

In a skillet over medium heat, add the bacon. Cook about 5 minutes or until the bacon is crisp. Remove the bacon from the skillet and drain on paper towels. Crumble the bacon into pieces.

Cut the turnip greens into 1" strips. Add the chopped onion, garlic, ginger and crushed red pepper flakes to the bacon drippings in the skillet. Stir frequently and cook for 3 minutes. Add the tomatoes and bring to a boil. Gradually stir in the turnip greens. Cook until the turnip greens wilt or about 3 minutes. Place a lid on the skillet and simmer for 10 minutes. Stir occasionally while the greens are cooking.

Stir in the great northern beans and remove the skillet from the heat. Preheat the oven to 350°. Spray a 1 1/2 quart casserole dish with non stick cooking spray. Spoon the mixture into the casserole dish. Sprinkle the cornbread over the top of the beans. Drizzle the butter over the cornbread. Bake for 25 minutes. Sprinkle the bacon over the top of the casserole. Bake for 5 minutes. Remove the dish from the oven and serve.

White Beans & Spinach

Makes 4 servings

16 cups fresh spinach, torn
4 tbs. water
4 garlic cloves, minced
1/2 tsp. salt
1/8 tsp. cayenne pepper
1/8 tsp. ground nutmeg
15 oz. can cannellini beans, rinsed and drained

In a large skillet over medium heat, add the spinach, water and garlic. Place a lid on the skillet and cook for 3 minutes. The spinach should be wilted and tender when ready. Stir the spinach occasionally to coat the spinach with the garlic.

Sprinkle the salt, cayenne pepper and nutmeg over the spinach. Toss until the spinach is seasoned. Stir in the cannellini beans and cook only until the beans are hot. Remove the skillet from the heat and serve.

Rosemary Cannellini Beans

Makes 4 servings

4 cups cooked cannellini beans
1/3 cup chicken broth
4 garlic cloves, finely minced
1 tsp. dried rosemary
1/8 tsp. salt
1/4 tsp. black pepper

Add all the ingredients to a sauce pan over medium heat. Stir frequently and cook for 5 minutes. The beans should be hot and the garlic tender when ready. Remove the pan from the heat and serve.

White Bean Hummus

Makes 3 cups

2 garlic cloves, peeled
1 tsp. chopped fresh rosemary
4 cups cooked great northern beans
3 tbs. lemon juice
3 tbs. tahini
3/4 tsp. salt
1/4 tsp. cayenne pepper
1/4 cup olive oil

Add the garlic and rosemary to a food processor. Pulse the food processor 4 times or until the garlic and rosemary are minced. Add the great northern beans, lemon juice, tahini, salt and cayenne pepper. Process until the mixture is combined and smooth. Scrape down the sides of the food processor if needed.

With the food processor running, slowly stream in the olive oil. Process until smooth. Spoon the hummus into a bowl. Cover the bowl and chill at least one hour before serving.

White Bean Spread

This is delicious over toasted bread or as a dip. I serve this as an appetizer over toasted bread rounds topped with fresh chopped tomatoes.

Makes 2 1/2 cups

1 cup dried white beans
Water
3 garlic cloves, peeled
1 tsp. dried rubbed sage
1 1/4 tsp. salt
1/2 tsp. black pepper
1/2 cup olive oil
7 oz. jar oil packed sun dried tomatoes, drained and chopped
1/2 cup chopped fresh parsley

Rinse the beans with cold water and remove any bad beans. Place the beans in a large sauce pan. Cover the beans with cold water about 2" above the beans. Place a lid on the pan and soak the beans for 8-12 hours. When the beans have soaked, drain off the soaking water. Rinse the beans with cold water and drain again.

Add 5 cups cold water, garlic, sage, 1 teaspoon salt and 1/4 teaspoon black pepper to the beans. Bring the beans to a boil over medium high heat. When the beans are boiling, place a lid on the pan and reduce the heat to medium low. Simmer the beans about 1 1/2 to 2 hours or until the beans are tender. Remove the beans from the stove. Drain off the bean liquid but save the bean liquid in a bowl. Discard the garlic cloves.

In a food processor bowl, add 1/4 of the beans. With the food processor running, slowly drizzle in the olive oil. Process until the bean mixture is smooth. Add the bean liquid as needed to make a smooth spread. Discard any remaining bean liquid.

Spoon the bean mixture into a bowl. Stir in 1/4 teaspoon salt, 1/4 teaspoon black pepper, sun dried tomatoes and parsley. You can add the remaining beans as needed to make the spread the consistency you desired. I usually mash about 1 cup of the remaining beans and add to the spread. Use any remaining beans for another use.

White Bean Dip

Makes 2 cups

This makes a lot but it will be gone in a flash. I serve this dip every holiday.

2 oz. can anchovies, drained and chopped
4 garlic cloves, minced
2 tbs. fresh rosemary, chopped
1 tbs. olive oil
2 cans drained cannellini beans, 15 oz. size
2 tbs. fresh lemon juice
A little more than 1/4 tsp. salt
A little more than 1/4 tsp. black pepper

In a small skillet over medium heat, add the anchovies, garlic, rosemary and olive oil. Saute the anchovies, rosemary and garlic for 2 minutes. Remove the skillet from the heat and set aside.

In a food processor, add the beans. Process the beans until smooth. Scrape down the sides of the food processor if needed. Add the anchovy mixture, lemon juice, salt and black pepper. Process until smooth.

Spoon the dip into a serving bowl. Serve with fresh vegetables or crackers. You can adjust the salt and black pepper to your taste.

White Bean Relish

Makes 2 cups

16 oz. can navy beans, drained and rinsed
1 cup finely chopped tomato
3/4 cup chopped red bell pepper
3/4 cup sliced green onions
1/2 cup finely chopped celery
2 tbs. fresh chopped cilantro
1 jalapeno pepper, seeded and chopped
1 garlic clove, minced
1 envelope dry Italian salad dressing mix
1/2 cup water
1/4 cup cider vinegar
1 tbs. olive oil

In a mixing bowl, add the navy beans, tomato, red bell pepper, green onions, celery, cilantro, jalapeno and garlic. In a glass jar with a lid, add the Italian dressing mix, water, cider vinegar and olive oil. Place the lid on the jar and shake until well combined.

Pour the dressing over the beans. Toss until combined. Use a slotted spoon and remove the relish from the dressing. Discard the dressing. Serve the relish with fish, seafood or most any meat.

7 GARBANZO BEANS

Garbanzo beans are also called chick peas. The beans are most famous for making hummus. Don't save these beans just for hummus, they are delicious in all types of casseroles and salads.

I find garbanzo beans taste best if cooked from dried peas. They are also cheaper to cook from dried peas. The broth from cooking the garbanzo beans is delicious. You can also use the broth as a substitute for chicken broth in some recipes.

Chickpea Chipotle Tostadas

Makes 6 servings

12 corn tortillas
Vegetable oil for frying
1 onion, chopped
1/2 cup red bell pepper, chopped
2 garlic cloves, chopped
1 tbs. olive oil
15 oz. can chickpeas, rinsed and drained
1 cup chicken broth
2 chipotle peppers in adobo sauce, minced
1/2 tsp. salt
2 tbs. fresh lime juice
1 cup sour cream
1/2 cup green chile sauce
3 cups shredded lettuce
6 plum tomatoes, chopped
1 cup crumbled feta cheese

In a deep skillet over medium heat, add vegetable oil to a depth of 2" in the skillet. When the oil is hot, fry the tortillas until crisp. Fry the tortillas one at a time to not overcrowd the skillet. Remove the tortillas from the skillet and drain on paper towels. Keep the tortillas warm while you prepare the rest of the dish.

In a skillet over medium high heat, add the onion, red bell pepper, garlic and olive oil. Saute the vegetables for 5 minutes. Stir in the chick peas, chicken broth, chipotle peppers and salt. Stir frequently and bring the chick peas to a boil. Reduce the heat to low and simmer for 5 minutes. Stir in the lime juice and cook for 2 minutes. You can mash the chick peas if desired. Remove the skillet from the heat.

Spoon the chickpeas over the tostadas. Top each tostada with sour cream, green chile sauce, lettuce, tomatoes and feta cheese.

Vegetarian Cassoulet

Makes 8 servings

1 lb. dried chickpeas
Water
3 tbs. minced garlic
1 bay leaf
1/4 cup unsalted butter
4 cups sliced fresh mushrooms
1/2 tsp. dried thyme
1/4 tsp. dried rosemary, crushed
1/2 tsp. dried oregano
1 cup dry white wine
3 tbs. tomato paste
6 turnips, peeled and cut into quarters
4 large red potatoes, peeled and cut into quarters
1 rutabaga, peeled and cut into 1" pieces
2 onions, peeled and cut into eight wedges per onion
6 carrots, peeled and cut into 2" pieces
1/2 tsp. salt
1/2 tsp. black pepper
1/4 cup olive oil
29 oz. can vegetable broth
1/2 cup fine dry breadcrumbs

In a 6 quart oven proof dutch oven, add the chickpeas. Add cold water to about 2" above the peas. Place a lid on the pot and soak the chickpeas for 8 hours. After the chickpeas have soaked, drain all the water from the chickpeas

Add 3 quarts cold water, 1 tablespoon garlic and the bay leaf to the pot. Place the pot over medium high heat. Bring the peas to a boil and reduce the heat to medium. Stir the peas frequently and cook the peas about 2 1/2 hours or until the peas are tender. Remove the pot from the heat. Remove the bay leaf and discard.

In a large skillet over medium heat, add the butter. When the butter melts, add 1 tablespoon garlic, mushrooms, thyme, rosemary and oregano. Stir constantly and cook for 5 minutes. Keep stirring and add the white wine and tomato paste. Cook for 2 minutes. Remove the skillet from the heat and add to the chickpeas in the pot. Stir until combined and set the chickpeas aside for now.

Vegetarian Cassoulet cont'd

Preheat the oven to 500°. Add 1 tablespoon garlic, turnips, potatoes, rutabaga, onions, carrots, salt, black pepper and olive oil to a roasting pan. Toss until combined. Bake for 20 minutes. Remove the roasting pan from the oven. Spoon the vegetables over the chickpeas in the pot.

Pour the vegetable broth over the top of the vegetables. Sprinkle the breadcrumbs over the top of the dish. Reduce the oven temperature to 325°. Bake for 1 to 1 1/2 hours or until the vegetables are tender. Remove the dish from the oven and serve.

Beef and Garbanzo Bean Dinner

Makes 4 servings

8 oz. ground beef
1/4 cup chopped onion
1/4 cup chopped green bell pepper
15 oz. can garbanzo beans, drained
15 oz. can stewed tomatoes, drained
1 tsp. ground cumin
1 tsp. chili powder
1/4 tsp. salt
1/8 tsp. black pepper
2 tbs. all purpose flour
3 tbs. water
1/4 cup shredded cheddar cheese
1 cup crushed tortilla chips

In a skillet over medium heat, add the ground beef, onion and green bell pepper. Stir frequently to break the ground beef into crumbles as it cooks. Cook about 6 minutes or until the ground beef is done and no longer pink. Drain off the excess grease.

Stir in the garbanzo beans, tomatoes, cumin, chili powder, salt and black pepper. Reduce the heat to low and simmer for 15 minutes. In a small bowl, stir together the all purpose flour and water. Add the flour to the ground beef. Stir until well combined and cook until the sauce thickens and bubbles. Remove the pan from the heat. Sprinkle the cheddar cheese over the top of the dish. Remove the skillet from the heat. Sprinkle the tortilla chips over the top before serving.

Red Pepper Hummus Pizza

Makes 6 servings

15 oz. can chickpeas, drained and rinsed
7 oz. jar roasted red bell pepper, chopped
2 garlic cloves, peeled
2 tbs. olive oil
1/2 tsp. salt
1/4 tsp. black pepper
10" Italian prebaked pizza crust
8 oz. pkg. crumbled feta cheese
3 plum tomatoes, sliced
1/4 cup black olives, sliced
1 tsp. dried oregano

Preheat the oven to 450°. Add the chickpeas, red bell pepper, garlic, olive oil, salt and black pepper to a blender. Process until smooth. Scrape down the sides of the blender if needed. Spread the mixture over the pizza crust.

Top the pizza with feta cheese, tomatoes, black olives and oregano. Bake for 10 minutes or until the pizza is lightly browned. Remove the pizza from the oven and serve. I use Boboli pizza crust for this pizza.

Garbanzo Bean Dip

Makes 1 3/4 cups

19 oz. can garbanzo beans, drained
1/2 cup prepared oil free Italian dressing
1 garlic clove
1 tbs. fresh lemon juice
Assorted raw vegetables

In a blender, add the garbanzo beans, Italian dressing, garlic and lemon juice. Process until well combined. Spoon the dip into a serving bowl. Cover the bowl and refrigerate until well chilled. Serve the dip with fresh raw vegetables.

Creamy Dried Tomato Hummus

Makes 2 cups

15 oz. can chickpeas, drained and rinsed
1 cup oil packed sun dried tomatoes, chopped
1 garlic clove, minced
1/2 cup mayonnaise
1/4 cup freshly grated Parmesan cheese
2 tbs. lemon juice
1/4 tsp. dried basil
1/8 tsp. cayenne pepper
1/8 cup chopped sun dried tomatoes, optional

In the bowl of a food processor, add the chickpeas, 1 cup sun dried tomatoes, garlic, mayonnaise, Parmesan cheese, lemon juice, basil and cayenne pepper. Process until smooth. Spoon the hummus into a serving dish. Garnish with 1/8 cup sun dried tomatoes if desired.

Quick Hummus

Makes 1 1/3 cups

2 garlic cloves, chopped
15 oz. can garbanzo beans, drained
1/4 cup tahini
2 tbs. lemon juice
2 tbs. water
1/4 tsp. salt

Add all the ingredients to the bowl of a food processor. Process until smooth. Store the hummus covered in the refrigerator. You can refrigerate the hummus before serving if desired.

Herbed Garbanzo Bean Spread

Makes 1 1/3 cups

15 oz. can garbanzo beans, drained
1 garlic clove, chopped
1 1/2 tbs. fresh lemon juice
1 tbs. olive oil
2 tsp. chopped fresh oregano
2 tsp. chopped fresh thyme
1/2 tsp. chili powder
1/4 tsp. salt
1/4 tsp. black pepper

Add all the ingredients to a food processor and process until smooth. Scrape down the sides of the bowl if needed. Remove the spread from the food processor and place in a small bowl. Chill if desired and serve with crackers.

Spaghetti with Garbanzo Bean Sauce

Makes 8 servings

1 onion, chopped
1 garlic clove, minced
1/2 cup chopped celery with leaves
3 tbs. olive oil
2 cups cooked garbanzo beans
Water
2 1/4 cups diced canned tomatoes with liquid
6 oz. can tomato paste
1 bay leaf
1 tsp. salt
1/8 tsp. cayenne pepper
1/2 tsp. dried oregano
1 lb. dry spaghetti noodles, hot and cooked
Grated Parmesan cheese, optional

In a large skillet over medium heat, add the onion, garlic, celery and olive oil. Saute the vegetables for 5 minutes. Drain the garbanzo beans but save the liquid in a large measuring cup. You need 2 1/2 cups liquid. Add water as needed to the garbanzo bean liquid to make 2 1/2 cups. Add the liquid, garbanzo beans, tomatoes with liquid, tomato paste, bay leaf, salt, cayenne pepper and oregano to the skillet. Stir until well combined.

Bring the sauce to a boil. When the sauce is boiling, reduce the heat to low. Stir the sauce occasionally and cook about 1-2 hours. The sauce should be thickened and combined when ready. Remove the skillet from the heat.

I find cooked dried garbanzo beans with liquid need to cook longer than 1 hour to make a good sauce. Canned garbanzo beans might be able to be cooked in 1 hour. The sauce should be thick and resemble commercial spaghetti sauce. Cook until the sauce is the consistency you like but no longer than 2 hours. Watch carefully so the sauce does not burn.

Place the hot spaghetti on a serving platter. Spoon the sauce over the spaghetti and top with Parmesan cheese if desired.

8 SALADS

Beans make a wonderful protein in salads. Whether you like your salads warm or cold, you will love these easy to fix bean salads. Included are a variety of bean salads. Most need to be prepared ahead of time. I love make ahead dishes that are ready to go when you get home from work.

Most of the salads use a homemade dressing but you can substitute your favorite salad dressing if desired.

Bean Salad Sandwiches

Makes 5 servings

2 cups cooked pinto beans, rinsed and drained
3 hard boiled eggs, chopped
1/2 cup chopped sweet pickle
2 tbs. chopped onion
3/4 tsp. salt
1/4 cup mayonnaise
5 pita pockets, halved
Lettuce as desired

In a mixing bowl, add the pinto beans. Mash the pinto beans with a fork or a potato masher. Mash to your desired consistency or leave some of the beans chunky. Add the eggs, sweet pickle, onion, salt and mayonnaise. Stir until combined. Cover the bowl and chill for 2 hours.

Line the pita pockets with lettuce if desired. Spoon the bean salad into the pita pockets and serve.

Mexican Chick Pea Salad

Makes 4 servings

2 cups cooked chick peas
1 jalapeno pepper, seeded and chopped
1/2 cup green bell pepper, chopped
1 red pimento, chopped
1 cup diced celery
2 tbs. capers
1/4 cup chopped green onions
1/4 cup olive oil
2 tbs. vinegar
Salt and black pepper to taste

In a serving bowl, add the chick peas, jalapeno pepper, green bell pepper, red pimento, celery, capers and green onions. In a separate bowl, whisk together the olive oil and vinegar. Pour the dressing over the salad. Toss until all the ingredients are combined. Season to taste with salt and black pepper.

You can serve the salad at room temperature or chilled.

Caribbean Shrimp Black Bean Salad

Makes 4 servings

15 oz. can black beans, drained and rinsed
1 green bell pepper, finely chopped
1/2 cup sliced celery
1/2 cup sliced purple onion, separated into rings
2 tbs. chopped fresh cilantro
2/3 cup picante sauce
1/4 cup lime juice
2 tbs. vegetable oil
2 tbs. honey
1/4 tsp. salt
2 lbs. medium size shrimp, cooked, peeled and deveined
Assorted lettuce leaves
Salt, black pepper or seafood seasoning to taste

In a mixing bowl, add the black beans, green bell pepper, celery, purple onion, cilantro, picante sauce, lime juice, vegetable oil, honey and salt. Stir until well combined. Cover the bowl and refrigerate for 8 hours.

The shrimp need to be chilled before serving. When ready to serve, place lettuce leaves on a serving plate. Spoon the black bean salad in the center of the lettuce leaves. Place the shrimp around the black bean salad. Season to taste with salt, black pepper or seafood seasoning.

White Bean Tuna Salad

Makes 8 servings

1 lb. dried great northern beans
Water
1 bay leaf
1 tsp. dried thyme
3 carrots, sliced
1 tbs. plus 1 tsp. salt
3/4 cup vegetable oil
1/4 cup red wine vinegar
1 1/2 tsp. dry mustard
1 tsp. ground coriander
1/4 tsp. black pepper
1 garlic clove, minced
1/2 cup chopped green onion
1 1/2 cups sliced celery
1/4 cup fresh minced parsley
4 cups romaine lettuce, chopped
3 cans drained and flaked tuna, 5 oz. size
1 cucumber, peeled and sliced
3 tomatoes, cut into wedges
12 black olives, halved

Place the beans in a large kettle. Cover the beans with cold water. Soak the beans for 5 hours. Drain the beans of the soaking water. Cover the beans with fresh cold water. Place the beans over medium heat and bring the beans to a boil. Add the bay leaf and thyme. Reduce the heat to medium low. Cook the beans for 2 hours. Add the carrots and 1 teaspoon salt. Cook until the beans and carrots are tender or about 1 hour.

Remove the beans from the heat and drain off all the liquid. Remove the bay leaf and discard. In a jar with a lid, add the vegetable oil, red wine vinegar, dry mustard, 1 tablespoon salt, coriander, black pepper and garlic. Place the lid on the jar and shake until well combined.

Place the beans in a large bowl. Pour the dressing over the beans. Add the green onion, celery and parsley. Toss to coat the beans with the dressing. Refrigerate for 4 hours before serving.

When ready to serve, add the lettuce to a large serving bowl. Spoon the beans and dressing over the lettuce. Top the beans with tuna, cucumbers, tomatoes and black olives.

Bean and Sausage Salad

Makes 6 servings

1 lb. cooked smoked sausage, sliced
1 onion, chopped
2 garlic cloves, minced
2 tbs. olive oil
4 cups cooked great northern beans
1 cup sliced black olives
7 oz. jar roasted red peppers, drained and chopped
1/3 cup red wine vinegar
1 tsp. Tabasco sauce
1/2 tsp. dried oregano
1 lb. fresh spinach, washed and stems removed

In a skillet over medium heat, add the smoked sausage, onion, garlic and olive oil. Saute the sausage and vegetables for 4 minutes. Drain off the excess grease if needed.

Stir in the great northern beans, black olives, red peppers, red wine vinegar, Tabasco sauce and oregano. Stir frequently and cook only until all the ingredients are thoroughly heated. Remove the skillet from the heat. Place the spinach on a serving plate. Spoon the warm sausage and bean salad over the spinach and serve.

Easy Marinated Pasta Bean Salad

This salad is so easy to make and is always a big hit at potlucks. Makes 10-12 servings

1/2 cup prepared Italian dressing
1/2 cup mayonnaise
1/2 tsp. cayenne pepper
1/2 tsp. dry mustard
8 oz. rotini pasta, cooked, drained and rinsed in cold water
15 oz. can great northern beans, drained and rinsed
15 oz. can black beans, drained and rinsed
15 oz. can kidney beans, drained and rinsed
8 oz. can whole kernel corn, drained and rinsed
2 oz. jar diced red pimentos, drained

Add the Italian dressing, mayonnaise, cayenne pepper and dry mustard to a large serving bowl. Stir until well combined. Add the pasta, great northern beans, black beans, kidney beans, corn and red pimentos. Toss until the beans and pasta are coated with the dressing. Cover the bowl with plastic wrap or a lid. Chill at least 3 hours before serving but no longer than 24 hours.

Spicy Bean Salad

Makes 6 servings

15 oz. can great northern beans, drained and rinsed
15 oz. can black beans, drained and rinsed
4 plum tomatoes, chopped
1 green bell pepper, chopped
3/4 cup chopped green onions
1/2 cup salsa
1/4 cup red wine vinegar
2 tbs. chopped fresh cilantro
1/2 tsp. salt
1/2 tsp. black pepper

Add all the ingredients to a large mixing bowl. Gently toss until well combined. Cover the bowl and refrigerate at least 2 hours before serving. Toss the salad again before serving.

Hoppin' John Salad

Makes 6 servings

2 celery stalks, diced
1 yellow bell pepper, chopped
1 red bell pepper, chopped
1/2 cup chopped onion
8 cups cooked black eye peas, rinsed
2 jalapeno peppers, seeded and diced
2 tbs. chopped fresh parsley
1 garlic clove, minced
1 tsp. salt
1 tsp. black pepper
1/2 tsp. ground cumin
1/2 cup red wine vinegar
2 tbs. balsamic vinegar
1/4 cup olive oil
4 bacon slices, cooked and crumbled

In a mixing bowl, add the celery, yellow bell pepper, red bell pepper, onion, black eye peas, jalapeno peppers, parsley, garlic, salt, black pepper and cumin. Toss until combined. In a small bowl, whisk together the red wine vinegar and balsamic vinegar. Keep whisking and slowly stream in the olive oil. Pour the dressing over the salad in the bowl. Toss until combined. Cover the bowl and chill for 4 hours before serving. Sprinkle the bacon over the top of the salad before serving.

Hominy Bean Salad

Makes 8 servings

15 oz. can yellow hominy, drained
16 oz. can red kidney beans, drained
1/4 cup sliced green onions
1/3 cup diced cucumber
1/4 cup diced red bell pepper
2 tbs. minced fresh parsley
3 tbs. vegetable oil
1/4 cup plus 1 tbs. cider vinegar
1 tbs. water
1/2 tsp. dried Italian seasoning
1 tsp. spicy brown mustard
1/8 tsp. celery seeds
1/4 tsp. chili powder
1/4 tsp. Tabasco sauce
1 cup alfalfa sprouts

In a mixing bowl, add the hominy, kidney beans, green onions, cucumber, red bell pepper and parsley. Toss until combined. In a mixing bowl, add the vegetable oil, cider vinegar, water, Italian seasoning, mustard, celery seeds, chili powder and Tabasco sauce. Whisk until well combined. Pour the dressing over the hominy and beans. Toss until all the ingredients are coated in the dressing. Cover the bowl with a lid or plastic wrap. Refrigerate for 8 hours.

When ready to serve, remove the vegetables and beans from the bowl using a slotted spoon. Place the vegetables and beans in a serving bowl. Sprinkle the alfalfa sprouts over the top before serving. You can pour the dressing left in the bowl over the alfalfa sprouts if desired.

Three Pea Salad

Makes 10 servings

16 oz. can garbanzo beans, drained and rinsed
16 oz. can black eye peas, drained and rinsed
16 oz. can green peas, drained
8 oz. jar cocktail onions with liquid
1/2 cup thinly sliced onion
1 green bell pepper, chopped
1/2 cup granulated sugar
1/2 cup vegetable oil
1/2 tsp. salt
1/4 tsp. black pepper

Add all the ingredients to a mixing bowl. Stir until well combined. Cover the bowl with a lid or plastic wrap. Refrigerate the salad overnight or at least 6 hours before serving. Toss the salad again before serving.

Chick Pea Salad

Makes 6 servings

3 tbs. olive oil
2 tbs. white wine vinegar
1/2 tsp. salt
1/2 tsp. black pepper
2 cans drained and rinsed chickpeas, 15 oz. size
3 green onions, chopped
1 cucumber, peeled, seeded and chopped
1/2 cup kalamata olives, chopped
3 plum tomatoes, chopped
1/4 cup chopped fresh parsley

In a small bowl, stir together the olive oil, white wine vinegar, salt and black pepper. Whisk until well blended. In a mixing bowl, add the chickpeas, green onions, cucumber, olives and tomatoes. Toss until blended. Pour the olive oil dressing over the salad. Toss until combined. Sprinkle the parsley over the top before serving.

Mediterranean Lentil Salad

Makes 4 servings

1 cup dried lentils
1 onion, chopped
1 qt. water
1 red bell pepper, chopped
1 green bell pepper, chopped
1 tomato, diced
3 green onions, diced
1/4 cup sliced black olives
1/2 cup prepared Italian salad dressing
1/2 tsp. black pepper
4 oz. tomato basil Feta cheese, crumbled

In a large sauce pan over medium heat, add the lentils, onion and water. Bring the lentils to a boil. When the lentils are boiling, reduce the heat to low and place a lid on the sauce pan. Simmer the lentils about 20 minutes or until the lentils are tender. Stir occasionally while the lentils are cooking. Remove the pan from the heat and drain all the liquid from the lentils.

Add the red bell pepper, green bell pepper, tomato, green onions, black olives, Italian salad dressing and black pepper to the lentils. Toss until well combined. Place a lid on the pan and refrigerate until well chilled. When ready to serve, spoon the lentils into a serving bowl and sprinkle the Feta cheese over the top.

Black Bean and Cheese Salad

Makes 4 servings

15 oz. can black beans, drained
4 oz. cheddar cheese, cut into 1/4" cubes
2 oz. jar diced red pimento, drained
2 tbs. minced onion
2 tbs. fresh lime juice
2 tbs. granulated sugar
1 tbs. vegetable oil
1/4 tsp. black pepper
4 lettuce leaves

In a mixing bowl, add the black beans, cheddar cheese, red pimento, onion, lime juice, granulated sugar, vegetable oil and black pepper. Toss until well combined. Place a lettuce leaf on each serving plate. Using a slotted spoon, remove the bean salad and place on each lettuce leaf.

Kidney Bean Coleslaw

Makes 8 servings

1/4 cup mayonnaise
3 tbs. chili sauce
1/4 tsp. celery seed
1/8 tsp. salt
3 cups shredded cabbage
1 cup cold, cooked kidney beans
1/4 cup sweet pickle relish
1/4 cup thinly sliced green onion

In a small bowl, add the mayonnaise, chili sauce, celery seed and salt. Stir until well combined. In a serving bowl, add the cabbage, kidney beans, pickle relish and green onions. Add the mayonnaise dressing to the bowl. Toss to coat the cabbage and beans with the dressing. Cover the bowl and refrigerate at least one hour before serving.

Bean Salad Vinaigrette

Makes 8 servings

1 cup olive oil
1/3 cup red wine vinegar
1 tsp. salt
1/8 tsp. black pepper
2 tbs. chopped capers
1/4 cup plus 2 tbs. chopped green onion
2 1/2 cups cooked chick peas
2 cups cooked carrots, sliced
2 cups cooked kidney beans
2 cups cooked white beans

In a jar with a lid, add the olive oil, red wine vinegar, salt, black pepper, capers and 2 tablespoons green onions. Place the lid on the jar and shake until well combined.

Place the chick peas, carrots, kidney beans and white beans in a serving bowl. Pour the dressing over the beans. Toss until the chick peas and beans are coated in the dressing. Refrigerate for 3 hours before serving. Sprinkle 1/4 cup green onions over the salad before serving.

Avocado Garbanzo Salad

Makes 4 servings

1/2 cup prepared French salad dressing
15 oz. can garbanzo beans, drained
1/4 head lettuce, chopped
1 avocado, peeled and quartered
1 tomato, cut into wedges
2 hard boiled eggs, quartered
1/4 cup pimento stuffed olives
1/2 cup shredded Monterey Jack cheese

In a mixing bowl, add the French dressing and garbanzo beans. Toss until combined. Cover the bowl and chill the garbanzo beans for 3 hours. Place the lettuce on a serving platter. Place the avocado, tomato wedges, hard boiled eggs and olives over the lettuce. Spoon the garbanzo beans and dressing over the lettuce. Sprinkle the Monterey Jack cheese over the top and serve.

Sweet & Sour Bean Salad

Makes 10 servings

2 lbs. fresh green beans, washed and stems removed
15 oz. can garbanzo beans, drained
1 purple onion, thinly sliced
4 oz. jar diced red pimento, drained
2/3 cup granulated sugar
1/2 cup vegetable oil
1/2 cup cider vinegar
1/2 cup tarragon wine vinegar
1 garlic clove, crushed
1/2 tsp. salt
1/2 tsp. lemon pepper seasoning

Cut the green beans into 1 1/2 " slices. Add the green beans to a sauce pan over medium heat. Cover the green beans with cold water. Bring the green beans to a boil and cook about 8 minutes. The green beans should be crisp tender. Remove the pan from the heat and drain all the water from the pan.

Add the green beans to a serving bowl. Stir in the garbanzo beans, onion and red pimento. In a glass jar with a lid, add the granulated sugar, vegetable oil, cider vinegar, tarragon wine vinegar, garlic, salt and lemon pepper seasoning. Place the lid on the jar and shake until well combined.

Pour the dressing over the vegetables. Toss until the vegetables and beans are coated. Cover the bowl with a lid or plastic wrap. Refrigerate at least 8 hours before serving. Toss the salad again before serving.

Full O' Beans Salad

Makes 6 servings

15 oz. can kidney beans, drained
15 oz. can garbanzo beans, drained
1/2 cup diced cheddar cheese
1/2 cup sliced celery
1/4 cup chopped onion
1/2 cup prepared Italian salad dressing
1/4 cup sweet pickle relish, drained
1/2 tsp. yellow prepared mustard
6 large lettuce leaves
6 bacon slices, cooked and crumbled

In a large bowl, add the kidney beans, garbanzo beans, cheddar cheese, celery and onion. Toss until combined. In a separate bowl, stir together the Italian salad dressing, pickle relish and mustard. Pour the dressing over the beans and toss until combined. Place a lettuce leaf on each serving plate. Spoon the bean salad over the lettuce leaves. Sprinkle the bacon over each salad and serve.

Pasta Bean Salad

Makes 4 servings

1/2 cup mayonnaise
1/4 cup minced fresh parsley
1/4 cup freshly grated Parmesan cheese
2 tbs. fresh lemon juice
1 garlic clove, finely minced
1 tsp. dried basil
2 cups cooked small pasta shells
15 oz. can red kidney beans, rinsed and drained
1 cup frozen green peas, thawed
1 cup diced carrots

In a small bowl, add the mayonnaise, parsley, Parmesan cheese, lemon juice, garlic and basil. Stir until well combined.

In a large serving bowl, add the pasta, kidney beans, green peas and carrots. Toss to combine the ingredients. Gently fold in the mayonnaise mixture. Fold until the salad is well combined and the pasta and beans are coated with the dressing. Cover the bowl and refrigerate for 2 hours before serving.

Four Bean Salad

Makes 12 servings

16 oz. can green beans, drained
16 oz. can golden wax beans, drained
15 oz. can lima beans, drained
15 oz. can red kidney beans, drained
1 green bell pepper, cut into 1" strips
1 onion, thinly sliced into rings
1 pt. cherry tomatoes, halved
1 cucumber, thinly sliced
1/2 cup red wine vinegar
1/2 cup vegetable oil
1/2 cup granulated sugar
1/2 tsp. dried tarragon
1/2 tsp. dried basil
2 tbs. minced fresh parsley
1/2 tsp. salt
1/2 tsp. dry mustard

In a large mixing bowl, add the green beans, golden wax beans, lima beans, red kidney beans, green bell pepper, onion, cherry tomatoes and cucumber.

In a glass jar with a lid, add the red wine vinegar, vegetable oil, granulated sugar, tarragon, basil, parsley, salt and dry mustard. Place the lid on the jar and shake until well blended. Pour the dressing over the vegetables in the mixing bowl. Toss until well blended. Cover the bowl and refrigerate at least 4 hours before serving.

Black Bean Salad

Makes 8 servings

4 cups cooked black beans
1 cup chopped fresh tomato
3/4 cup chopped red bell pepper
2/3 cup sliced green onion
1/2 cup chopped celery
1 tbs. lemon zest
1 garlic clove, minced
2 tbs. minced fresh cilantro
1 envelope dry Italian salad dressing mix
3/4 cup water
1/4 tsp. cayenne pepper
2 tbs. olive oil

Add the black beans, tomato, red bell pepper, green onion, celery, lemon zest, garlic and cilantro to a serving bowl. Toss until combined. In a jar with a lid, add the dry Italian dressing mix, water, cayenne pepper and olive oil. Place the lid on the jar and shake until well combined.

Pour the dressing over the beans and vegetables in the bowl. Gently toss to combine the dressing with the beans and vegetables. Cover the bowl with a lid or plastic wrap. Refrigerate the salad until well chilled. Toss the salad again before serving.

Black Bean and Rice Salad

Makes 8 servings

2 tbs. orange juice
2 tsp. lemon juice
2 tsp. olive oil
1/2 tsp. salt
1/2 tsp. ground cumin
1/2 tsp. Tabasco sauce
1 cup cooked rice
4 cups cooked black beans, rinsed and drained
3 plum tomatoes, seeded and chopped
1 red bell pepper, chopped
1/2 cup green bell pepper, chopped
1/2 cup purple onion, chopped
1/4 cup diced celery

In a large bowl, add the orange juice, lemon juice, olive oil, salt, cumin and Tabasco sauce. Whisk until well combined. Stir in the rice, black beans, tomatoes, red bell pepper, green bell pepper, purple onion and celery. Toss until well combined. Cover the bowl and refrigerate at least 1 hour before serving.

Black Bean and Barley Salad

Makes 4 servings

1/4 cup fresh lime juice
2 tbs. water
1 tbs. vegetable oil
1 tsp. granulated sugar
1/2 tsp. garlic powder
1/4 tsp. salt
1/4 tsp. black pepper
1/4 tsp. ground cumin
1/4 tsp. cayenne pepper
3/4 cup barley, cooked and cooled
15 oz. can black beans, drained and rinsed
1 cup chopped tomato
1/2 cup shredded cheddar cheese
1/4 cup sliced green onion

In a jar with a lid, add the lime juice, water, vegetable oil, granulated sugar, garlic powder, salt, black pepper, cumin and cayenne pepper. Place the lid on the jar and shake until well combined.

In a serving bowl, add the cooled barley. Pour half the dressing over the barley. Cover the bowl and refrigerate for 8 hours. Stir occasionally to keep the barley covered in the dressing. Add the black beans, tomato, cheddar cheese, green onion and the remaining dressing to the salad. Toss to coat the ingredients and serve.

Kidney Bean Wild Rice Salad

Makes 8 servings

1 cup chicken broth
1 cup orange juice
1/3 cup water
6 oz. pkg. long grain & wild rice mix
4 cups cooked kidney beans
3 hard boiled eggs, diced
1 onion, minced
1/2 cup mayonnaise
1/4 tsp. salt
1/4 tsp. black pepper
1/8 tsp. cayenne pepper
1/2 cup sliced almonds, toasted
1/4 cup minced fresh parsley, optional

In a sauce pan over medium heat, add the chicken broth, orange juice and water. Bring the liquids to a boil. Stir in the rice and bring the rice back to a boil. Place a lid on the pan and reduce the heat to low. Simmer the rice about 25-30 minutes or until the rice is tender. Remove the pan from the heat.

Stir in the kidney beans, eggs, onion, mayonnaise, salt, black pepper and cayenne pepper. Cover the pan and chill for 2 hours. Stir the salad again before serving. Sprinkle the almonds and parsley over the top of the salad and serve.

Quick Bean Salad

Makes 6 servings

15 oz. can garbanzo beans, drained
16 oz. can French style green beans, drained
14 oz. can artichoke hearts, drained and quartered
1/2 cup bottled Italian salad dressing

Add the garbanzo beans, green beans and artichokes to a serving bowl. Toss until combined. Pour the Italian dressing over the vegetables. Toss until the dressing coats the salad ingredients. Cover the bowl and refrigerate the salad until chilled. Drain off the dressing before serving if desired.

Chickpea and Fennel Salad

Makes 8 servings

6 tbs. olive oil
3 tbs. white wine vinegar
3/4 tsp. black pepper
1/2 tsp. salt
1/2 tsp. dried thyme
1/2 tsp. crushed red pepper flakes
4 cups cooked chickpeas, drained and rinsed
2 fennel bulbs, thinly sliced
3 garlic cloves, minced
1/2 cup crumbled Gorgonzola cheese
1/4 cup minced fresh parsley

Add the olive oil, white wine vinegar, black pepper, salt, thyme and red pepper flakes to a serving bowl. Whisk until well combined. Add the chickpeas, fennel and garlic. Toss until all the ingredients are well combined. Cover the bowl and chill at least 1 hour. Sprinkle the Gorgonzola cheese and parsley over the top before serving.

Pinto Bean Salad

Makes 8 servings

4 cups cooked pinto beans
4 hard boiled eggs, chopped
1 cup shredded Monterey Jack cheese
1/2 cup sliced purple onion
1/2 cup vegetable oil
2 tbs. cider vinegar
2 tbs. red wine vinegar
2 tbs. picante sauce
1 tbs. plus 1 tsp. Dijon mustard
8 lettuce leaves
4 slices cooked bacon, crumbled

In a serving bowl, add the pinto beans, eggs, Monterey Jack cheese and purple onion. Toss until well combined. In a glass jar with a lid, add the vegetable oil, cider vinegar, red wine vinegar, picante sauce and Dijon mustard. Place the lid on the jar and shake until well combined. Pour the dressing over the bean mixture. Toss until well combined and all the ingredients are coated with the dressing.

Place the lettuce leaves on a serving platter. Spoon equal amounts of the bean salad on each lettuce leaf. Sprinkle the crumbled bacon over the top and serve.

Black Eye Pea Salad

Makes 8 servings

4 cups cooked black eye peas
1/2 cup chopped red onion
1/2 cup chopped green bell pepper
1/2 clove garlic
1/4 cup vinegar
1/4 cup granulated sugar
1/4 cup vegetable oil
1/2 tsp. salt
1/8 tsp. black pepper
Dash of Tabasco sauce

In a serving bowl, add the black eye peas, red onion, green bell pepper and garlic. Toss until combined. In a small bowl, add the vinegar, granulated sugar, vegetable oil, salt, black pepper and Tabasco sauce. Whisk until well combined.

Pour the dressing over the black eye peas. Toss until well coated. Cover the bowl and refrigerate at least 12 hours before serving. Remove the garlic clove before serving.

Mexican Black Eye Pea Salad

Makes 8 servings

3/4 cup dried black eye peas
Water
1 lb. ground beef
1 onion, chopped
1/2 cup chopped green bell pepper
1 tbs. chili powder
1/2 tsp. salt
1/8 tsp. black pepper
1 head lettuce, torn into bite size pieces
2 tomatoes, peeled and chopped
2 avocados, peeled and chopped
1 cup shredded cheddar cheese
1 cup cooked whole kernel corn
4 cups crushed tortilla chips
1/2 cup prepared Thousand Island dressing
1/2 cup prepared creamy Italian dressing

Rinse the black eye peas with cold water. Place the peas in a large sauce pan over medium heat. Cover the peas with cold water to about 2" above the peas. Bring the peas to a boil and boil for 2 minutes. Remove the peas from the heat and place a lid on the pan. Let the peas soak for 1 hour. When the peas have soaked, drain the water from the peas.

Add 2 1/2 cups fresh cold water to the peas. Place the peas back on the stove over medium heat and bring the peas to a boil. When the peas are boiling, reduce the heat to low. Place a lid on the pan and simmer for 1 to 1 1/2 hours or until the peas are tender. Remove the peas from the heat and cool completely before using.

In a skillet over medium heat, add the ground beef, onion and green bell pepper. Stir frequently to break the meat into crumbles as it cooks. Cook for 6-7 minutes or until the ground beef is done and no longer pink. Drain off the excess grease. Stir in the chili powder, salt and black pepper. Remove the pan from the heat and let the ground beef cool before using.

In a large bowl, add the black eye peas, ground beef, lettuce, tomatoes, avocados, cheddar cheese, corn and tortilla chips. Drizzle the Thousand Island dressing and the Italian dressing over the salad. Toss until well combined and serve immediately.

Goat Cheese & Black Eye Pea Salad

Makes 6 servings

6 oz. goat cheese
1 1/4 cups olive oil
1 1/2 tsp. dried thyme
1/2 tsp. dried tarragon
8 oz. dried black eye peas
3 cups water
1 small smoked ham hock
1 bay leaf
2 garlic cloves, minced
1/2 tsp. salt
1 purple onion, cut into thin slices
1 red bell pepper, cut into 1/4" strips
1/4 cup dry breadcrumbs
1/3 cup red wine vinegar
1 tsp. dry mustard
1 tsp. dried oregano
2 tsp. honey
8 cups mixed salad greens

Cut the goat cheese into 6 slices. Place the slices in a shallow bowl. Drizzle 1/4 cup olive oil over the cheese. Sprinkle 1/2 teaspoon thyme and the tarragon over the cheese. Cover the dish and chill for 8 hours.

In a sauce pan over medium heat, add the black eye peas, water, ham hock, bay leaf, garlic and salt. Stir to combine the ingredients and bring the peas to a boil. When the peas are boiling, reduce the heat to low and place a lid on the pan. Simmer for 1 hour or until the peas are tender. Remove the pan from the heat. Remove the bay leaf and discard.

Remove the ham hock and cut the meat from the hock. Add the meat back to the peas. Set the peas aside for the moment. In a skillet over medium heat, add the onion and red bell pepper. Stir constantly and cook about 6 minutes. The onion and red bell pepper should be slightly browned. Remove the skillet from the heat.

Place the breadcrumbs in a shallow bowl. Preheat the oven to 350°. Dredge the goat cheese slices in the breadcrumbs. Place the slices on a baking sheet. Bake for 10 minutes.

Goat Cheese & Black Eye Pea Salad cont'd

To make the vinaigrette, add the red wine vinegar, dry mustard, oregano, 1 teaspoon thyme and honey to a food processor. Pulse 4 times. With the food processor running, slowly add 1 cup olive oil. Process until blended.

When ready to serve, place the salad greens on a large platter. Spoon the black eye peas over the greens. Spoon the onion and red bell pepper over the peas. Place the goat cheese slices over the top. Drizzle the vinaigrette over the top of the salad and serve.

Curry Black Eye Pea Salad

Makes 4 servings

2 cups black eye peas
1/2 cup sliced green onions
1/2 cup chopped yellow bell pepper
1 garlic clove, minced
1 1/4 tsp. grated lemon zest
1/4 tsp. plus 1/8 tsp. black pepper
2 tbs. lemon juice
1/2 cup plain yogurt
1 tbs. pineapple juice
1 1/4 tsp. curry powder
1/4 tsp. salt
2 tbs. dry roasted cashews

In a serving bowl, add the black eye peas, green onions, yellow bell pepper, garlic, lemon zest, 1/4 teaspoon black pepper and lemon juice. Toss until well combined. Cover the bowl and chill for 1 hour.

In a small bowl, add the yogurt, pineapple juice, curry powder, salt and 1/8 teaspoon black pepper. Stir until well combined. Cover the bowl and chill at least 1 hour.

When ready to serve, add the yogurt dressing to the black eye peas. Toss until all the ingredients are well coated. Sprinkle the cashews over the top and serve.

Black Eye Pea Vinaigrette Salad

Makes 10 servings

1 lb. dried black eye peas
Water
1 onion, chopped
2 garlic cloves, minced
3 bay leaves
2 tsp. salt
2 tsp. ground cumin
1 tsp. dried marjoram
1/2 cup plus 2 tbs. vegetable oil
1/4 cup red wine vinegar
3 tbs. minced fresh parsley
2 tbs. dried cilantro
1 tsp. black pepper

Wash the black eye peas in cold water and remove any bad peas. Add the peas to a large pot. Add the water, onion, garlic, bay leaves, salt, cumin and marjoram. Place the pot over medium heat and bring the peas to a boil. When the peas are boiling, reduce the heat to low and place a lid on the pot. Simmer the peas for 1 to 2 hours. The peas should be tender but not mushy when ready. Remove the pot from the heat and remove the bay leaves. Drain all the water from the peas.

In a small bowl, add the vegetable oil, red wine vinegar, parsley, cilantro and black pepper. Whisk until well combined and add to the peas. Stir until combined. Let the peas cool for 20 minutes. Serve the salad at room temperature.

Black Eye Pea Sweet Potato Salad

Makes 8 servings

2 sweet potatoes, peeled and cubed
1 tbs. vegetable oil
1 purple onion, quartered and thinly sliced
2 garlic cloves, minced
1 tsp. dried basil
1 tsp. dried thyme
1/2 tsp. ground cumin
1/2 tsp. ground coriander
1/3 cup lime juice
1/2 cup mango chutney
6 cups cooked black eye peas, rinsed and drained
1/2 cup chopped fresh parsley
1 tsp. salt
1 tsp. black pepper

In a sauce pan over medium heat, add the sweet potatoes. Cover the sweet potatoes with water. Bring the sweet potatoes to a boil and simmer the sweet potatoes about 15 minutes. The sweet potatoes should be tender but not mushy. You need the sweet potatoes to hold their shape. Do not over cook the sweet potatoes. If you stick a fork in the sweet potato, it should be tender and not fall apart when done. Remove the pan from the heat and drain all the water from the pan.

In a sauce pan over medium heat, add the vegetable oil and purple onion. Saute the onion for 4 minutes. Add the garlic, basil, thyme, cumin and coriander. Stir constantly and cook for 2 minutes. Remove the pan from the heat.

In a large bowl, add the lime juice and mango chutney. Stir until well combined. Add the sweet potatoes, onion mixture, black eye peas, parsley, salt and black pepper. Gently toss until well combined. Cover the bowl and chill at least 2 hours before serving.

Bean Relish

Makes 6 servings

This is great by itself or served over lettuce.

1 cup granulated sugar
3/4 cup vinegar
1/2 cup vegetable oil
1 tsp. salt
1 tsp. black pepper
2 cups cooked sliced green beans
2 cups whole kernel corn, cooked
2 cups cooked green peas
1 green bell pepper, chopped
1 onion, chopped
1/2 cup celery, chopped

In a sauce pan over medium low heat, add the granulated sugar, vinegar, vegetable oil, salt and black pepper. You only need to heat the dressing until the sugar dissolves. Do not let the dressing boil. Remove the pan from the heat.

In a serving bowl with a lid, add the green beans, corn, green peas, green bell pepper, onion and celery. Pour the warm dressing over the vegetables. Toss to coat the vegetables. Place the lid on the bowl and marinate for 24 hours before serving.

9 BLACK EYE PEAS

Black eye peas are a southern tradition. We eat them all year long but they are a must have on New Year's day. We grow them in our gardens or use dried peas all year long. Black eye peas make a wonderful dip. Black eye pea dips and spreads are served at most southern parties. Try the wide variety of black eye pea recipes included in this cookbook.

When I was a kid, Aunt Violet made the most wonderful fresh black eye peas with biscuits. She would add diced bacon to the black eye peas while cooking. She would cook them slowly and they would produce a rich pea broth. I loved to spoon the pea broth over biscuits.

Zesty Black Eye Pea Relish

Makes 7 cups

4 cups cooked black eye peas
1 cup chopped celery
1 green bell pepper, chopped
1 large tomato, peeled and chopped
2 garlic cloves, minced
2 green onions, sliced
4 oz. jar sliced mushrooms, drained
4 oz. jar diced red pimentos, drained
1 cup Italian salad dressing
1/2 tsp. black pepper

Add all the ingredients to a glass bowl. Stir until well combined. Place a lid on the bowl and refrigerate at least 5 hours before serving. Drain the relish before serving. The relish will keep up to 1 week covered in the refrigerator.

Pickled Black Eye Peas

Makes 5 cups

2 cans rinsed and drained black eye peas, 16 oz. size
2/3 cup vegetable oil
1/3 cup white wine vinegar
1 cup diced onion
1 garlic clove, minced
1/2 tsp. salt
1/8 tsp. black pepper

Add all the ingredients to a glass mixing bowl. Stir until combined. Cover the bowl and chill at least 2 hours. Serve with tortilla chips if desired.

Plain Ole Black Eye Peas

Makes 6 cups

Not only are the peas delicious in this recipe, but use the peas in recipes for other dishes. I have included our favorite recipes in this book for using Plain Ole Black Eye Peas.

1 lb. pkg. dried black eye peas
Water
4 slices bacon
1 tbs. salt
1 tbs. granulated sugar
1 tbs. white wine vinegar
1/4 tsp. black pepper
1/4 tsp. garlic salt

Rinse the peas in cold water and remove any bad peas. Place the peas in a dutch oven. Cover the peas with cold water about 2" above the peas. Place a lid on the dutch oven and soak the peas for 8 hours.

When the peas have soaked, drain the peas. Add 6 cups cold water, bacon, salt, granulated sugar, white wine vinegar, black pepper and garlic salt to the peas. Place the pot over medium heat and bring the peas to a boil. When the peas are boiling, place a lid on the pot and reduce the heat to low. Simmer the peas for 1 1/2 to 2 hours or until the peas are tender. Remove the pot from the heat and serve.

Chinese Black Eye Peas

Makes 8 servings

2 tsp. unsalted butter, melted
8 green onions, sliced
8 oz. can sliced water chestnuts, drained
8 oz. can bamboo shoots, drained
1/2 tsp. instant chicken bouillon granules
1 tsp. teriyaki sauce
1 tsp. soy sauce
4 cups Plain Ole Black Eye Peas (recipe in this book)
Salt and black pepper to taste
8 green onions, cut into small strips

In a skillet over medium heat, add 1 teaspoon melted butter and 8 sliced green onions. Saute the onion about 4 minutes or until the onions are crisp tender. Stir in the water chestnuts, bamboo shoots, chicken bouillon granules, teriyaki sauce and soy sauce. Stir constantly and cook until all the ingredients are hot and combined. Add the black eye peas and season to taste with salt and black pepper. Simmer until the peas are hot.

In a skillet over medium heat, add 1 teaspoon melted butter and 8 green onions that have been cut into strips. Saute the green onions for 4 minutes. Remove the skillet from the heat. Place the peas in a serving bowl and sprinkle the green onion strips over the top before serving.

Cajun Peas

Makes 8 servings

3 cups cooked long grain rice
1 cup sour cream
1 tsp. poultry seasoning
2 cups cooked red beans
2 cups Plain Ole Black Eye Peas (recipe in this book)
1/2 cup diced cooked smoked sausage
1/2 cup shredded Monterey Jack cheese

Spray a 2 quart casserole dish with non stick cooking spray. Preheat the oven to 350°. Add the rice to the casserole dish. In a small bowl, stir together the sour cream and poultry seasoning. Spread the sour cream over the rice in the casserole dish.

Spoon the red beans and black eye peas over the sour cream. Bake for 30 minutes. Sprinkle the smoked sausage and Monterey Jack cheese over the top of the dish. Bake for 10 minutes. The sausage should be hot and the cheese melted when ready. Remove the dish from the oven and serve.

Baked Sweet & Sour Peas

Makes 8 servings

8 cups Plain Ole Black Eye Peas (recipe in this book)
1 1/2 cups plus 2 tsp. sweet and sour sauce
8 oz. can crushed pineapple, drained
1/3 cup chopped green onions

Preheat the oven to 350°. Spray a 2 quart casserole dish with non stick cooking spray. Add the black eye peas and 1 1/2 cups sweet and sour sauce to the casserole dish. Stir until combined and the peas are coated with the sauce.

In a small bowl, stir together the crushed pineapple and 2 teaspoon sweet and sour sauce. Spoon the mixture over the top of the peas. Sprinkle the green onions over the top. Bake for 30 minutes or until the dish is hot and bubbly.

Black Eye Pea Cakes

Makes about 15 cakes

1 onion, chopped
1 tbs. olive oil
4 cups cooked black eye peas
8 oz. container chive and onion cream cheese, softened
1 egg
1/2 tsp. salt
1 tsp. Tabasco sauce
8 oz. pkg. hush puppy mix
Olive oil for frying

In a skillet over medium heat, add the onion and 1 tablespoon olive oil. Saute the onion for 4 minutes or until the onion is tender. Remove the skillet from the heat. Add the onion, 2 cups black eye peas, cream cheese, egg, salt and Tabasco sauce to a blender. Pulse until the mixture is combined and smooth. Scrape down the sides of the blender if needed.

Stir in the hush puppy mix and 2 cups black eye peas. Using about 4 tablespoons of the pea mixture, form into patties. Place the patties on a wax paper lined baking sheet. Cover the patties with plastic wrap. Chill the patties at least 1 hour or until firm.

When ready to cook, add enough olive oil to cover the bottom of a skillet. Heat the oil over medium heat. You will have to cook the patties in batches. Place as many patties as you can in the skillet. Fry about 3 minutes on each side or until the patties are golden brown. Remove the patties from the heat and serve.

Add olive oil as needed to fry all the patties. Keep the patties warm while you finish cooking all the patties. I heat my oven to 200° and place the patties on a platter to keep them warm.

Black Eye Pea Spaghetti

Makes 8 servings

1 cup elbow macaroni
6 cups water
1 cup chopped onions
3 garlic cloves, minced
1 lb. ground beef
2 cans diced stewed tomatoes, 16 oz. size
1 1/2 tsp. chili seasoning
1 tsp. season salt
2 tsp. garlic salt
1/2 tsp. ground oregano
1/2 tsp. dried basil
1 1/2 tsp. granulated sugar
1 tsp. salt
1/4 tsp. black pepper
1 tbs. Worcestershire sauce
5 cups frozen black eye peas, cooked

In a large sauce pan over medium heat, add the water. Bring the water to a boil. When the water boils, add the elbow macaroni. Cook for 6-7 minutes or until the macaroni is tender. Remove the pan from the heat and drain all the water from the macaroni.

In a skillet over medium heat, add the onions, garlic and ground beef. Stir frequently to break the meat into crumbles as it cooks. Cook for 6-7 minutes or until the ground beef is done and no longer pink. Drain off the excess grease.

Stir in the tomatoes with liquid, chili seasoning, season salt, garlic salt, oregano, basil, granulated sugar, salt, black pepper and Worcestershire sauce. Stir frequently and cook for 25 minutes. If the liquid is evaporating too fast, reduce the heat to low. Stir in the cooked macaroni and black eye peas. Cook for 5 minutes. Remove the skillet from the heat and serve.

Mexican Bean & Black Eye Pea Casserole

Makes 8 servings

2/3 cup chopped onion
1 tbs. unsalted butter, melted
2/3 cup chopped green bell pepper
1 tomato, peeled and chopped
2 tsp. chopped jalapeno pepper
1/2 cup mild taco sauce
4 cups Plain Ole Black Eye Peas (recipe in this book)
15 oz. can Mexican style chili beans
1 cup shredded cheddar cheese
1 cup sour cream, optional

Preheat the oven to 350°. Spray a 2 quart baking dish with non stick cooking spray. In a skillet over medium heat, add the onion and melted butter. Saute the onion for 3 minutes. Add the green bell pepper, tomato, jalapeno pepper and 1/4 cup taco sauce. Stir until well combined and thoroughly heated. Remove the skillet from the heat.

Add the black eye peas, chili beans and 1/4 cup taco sauce to the casserole dish. Stir until well combined. Spoon the onion and peppers mixture over the top of the beans and peas. Bake for 25 minutes or until the dish is hot and bubbly.

Sprinkle the cheddar cheese over the top and bake for 10 minutes. The cheese should be melted and bubbly when ready. Remove the dish from the oven and serve. Spread the sour cream over the top if desired.

Marinated Black Eye Peas

Makes 5 cups

4 cups cooked black eye peas
2/3 cup olive oil
1 cup diced purple onion
1/3 cup white wine vinegar
1 garlic clove, minced
1/2 tsp. salt
1 tsp. black pepper
2 cups cooked whole kernel corn
1 minced jalapeno pepper
1/2 cup chopped red bell pepper

Add all the ingredients to a glass bowl. Stir until well combined. Cover the bowl and chill at least 4 hours. I like to serve the peas over lettuce leaves.

Black Eye Pea Skillet Dinner

Makes 6 servings

1 lb. ground beef
1 1/4 cups chopped onion
1 cup chopped green bell pepper
4 cups cooked black eye peas
16 oz. can whole tomatoes
3/4 tsp. salt
1/2 tsp. black pepper

In a skillet over medium heat, add the ground beef, onion and green bell pepper. Stir frequently to break the meat into crumbles as it cooks. Cook for 7-8 minutes or until the ground beef is well browned and no longer pink. Drain off the excess grease.

Stir in the black eye peas, tomatoes with juice, salt and black pepper. Bring the mixture to a boil. Reduce the heat to low and place a lid on the skillet. Simmer for 30 minutes. Stir frequently as the dish cooks to prevent burning and to break the tomatoes up into pieces as they cook. Remove the skillet from the heat and serve.

Black Eye Peas & Ham Hocks

Makes 12 servings

3 cups dried black eye peas
Water
3 lbs. smoked ham hocks
1 1/4 cups chopped onion
1 cup chopped green bell pepper
2 bay leaves
16 oz. can stewed tomatoes, chopped
1 tsp. salt

Rinse the black eye peas with cold water and add to a stock pot. Cover the peas with cold water about 2" above the peas. Place a lid on the pot and soak the peas for 8 hours. When the peas have soaked, drain all the water from the peas.

Add 6 cups fresh cold water, ham hocks, onion, green bell pepper and bay leaves to the peas. Place the pot over medium high heat and bring the peas to a boil. When the peas are boiling, reduce the heat to medium low. Place a lid on the pot and simmer the peas for 1 hour. The peas should be almost done at this point.

Stir in the stewed tomatoes and salt. Simmer the peas about 15 minutes or until the peas are tender. Remove the ham hocks from the peas. Cut the meat from the hocks and discard the fat and bones. Add the meat back to the pot. Remove the bay leaves and discard. Remove the pot from the heat and serve.

Special Black Eye Peas

Makes 8 servings

3 slices bacon
2 celery stalks, sliced
1 onion, chopped
2 tbs. chopped green bell pepper
16 oz. can diced tomatoes
1 1/2 cups water
2 pkgs. frozen black eye peas, 10 oz. size
1 tsp. Worcestershire sauce
1/2 tsp. salt
1/4 tsp. black pepper
1 bay leaf

In a large sauce pan over medium heat, add the bacon. Cook the bacon for 6-7 minutes or until the bacon is crisp. Remove the bacon from the pan but leave the bacon drippings in the pan. Drain the bacon on paper towels. Crumble the bacon into pieces.

Add the celery, onion and green bell pepper to the pan. Saute the vegetables for 5 minutes. Stir in the tomatoes, water, black eye peas, Worcestershire sauce, salt, black pepper and bay leaf. Bring the peas to a boil. Place a lid on the pan and reduce the heat to low. Simmer for 1 hour or until the peas are tender. Remove the bay leaf from the pan and discard. Sprinkle the crumbled bacon over the top before serving.

Creole Black Eye Peas

Makes 6 servings

4 slices bacon
1 cup chopped onion
1 cup chopped green bell pepper
1 cup chopped celery
14 oz. can diced tomatoes, drained
16 oz. can black eye peas, drained
2 tsp. granulated sugar
1 bay leaf

In a skillet over medium heat, add the bacon. Cook the bacon for 6-7 minutes or until the bacon is crispy. Remove the bacon from the skillet and drain on paper towels. Leave the bacon drippings in the skillet. Crumble the bacon into pieces.

Add the onion, green bell pepper and celery to the bacon drippings. Saute the vegetables about 5 minutes. Stir in the tomatoes, black eye peas, granulated sugar and the bay leaf. Reduce the heat to low. Stir occasionally and cook about 15 minutes. Remove the skillet from the heat. Remove the bay leaf and discard. Spoon the peas into a serving bowl. Sprinkle the crumbled bacon over the top before serving.

Black Eye Pea & Spinach Stuffed Potatoes

Makes 6 servings

6 large baking potatoes
10 oz. pkg. frozen spinach, thawed
15 oz. can black eye peas, drained
16 oz. can diced tomatoes, drained
1/2 cup chopped red bell pepper
1/4 cup chopped onion
1 tbs. minced fresh cilantro
3 tbs. lime juice
1 tbs. olive oil
1 garlic clove, minced
1/2 tsp. ground cumin
1/4 tsp. salt
Dash of Tabasco sauce

Wash and scrub the potatoes. Prick each potato with a fork. Preheat the oven to 400°. Place the potatoes in the oven and bake for 1 hour or until the potatoes are tender. Remove the potatoes from the oven.

All moisture must be removed from the spinach. Pat the spinach with paper towels if needed to remove the moisture. In a sauce pan over medium heat, add the spinach, black eye peas, tomatoes, red bell pepper, onion, cilantro, lime juice, olive oil, garlic, cumin, salt and Tabasco sauce. Stir until well combined and bring the peas to a boil. Remove the pan from the heat.

Split the potatoes open and spoon the spinach pea mixture over the top of each potato to serve.

Spicy Black Eye Peas

Makes 8 servings

1 lb. bag dried black eye peas
Water
2 tbs. minced green onions
1 tbs. Creole seasoning
1 tsp. dried parsley flakes
1 tsp. garlic powder
1 tsp. chili powder
1 tsp. black pepper
3 chicken bouillon cubes

Wash the black eye peas in cold water. Place the peas in a large dutch oven. Cover the black eye peas with cold water about 2" above the peas. Place a lid on the pot and soak the peas for 8 hours. Drain all the water from the peas.

Add 5 cups fresh cold water, green onions, Creole seasoning, parsley flakes, garlic powder, chili powder, black pepper and chicken bouillon to the pot. Place the peas over medium heat and bring the peas to a boil. Reduce the heat to low and place a lid on the pot. Stir occasionally and simmer the peas for 1 to 1 1/2 hours or until the peas are tender.

Add a cup or two of water if needed to the peas while cooking. Do not add too much additional water as this will water down the spices. You only need to keep the peas lightly covered in water. Remove the peas from the heat and serve.

Old Fashioned Hopping John

Makes 12 servings

2 lbs. dried black eye peas
Water
2 ham hocks
2 tsp. salt
4 1/2 cups cooked rice
Salt, black pepper & Tabasco sauce to taste

Wash and rinse the dried peas. Remove any bad peas. Add the peas to a dutch oven over medium heat. Cover the peas with cold water and bring the peas to a boil. Boil for 3 minutes. Remove the pot from the heat and place a lid on the pot. Let the peas sit for 1 hour.

Add the ham hocks and salt to the peas. Place the peas back on the stove over medium heat. Bring the peas to a boil and reduce the heat to medium low. Place a lid on the pot but the lid needs to be ajar on the pot. You need the steam to escape. Add water as needed to keep the peas and ham hocks covered in water. Cook about 1 to 1 1/2 hours or until the peas are tender.

Remove the ham hocks from the pot. Pull the meat on the hocks from the bone. Add the pulled meat back to the pot. Stir in the cooked rice. Heat only until the rice is warmed. Season to taste with additional salt, black pepper and Tabasco sauce if desired.

Black Eye Peas with Pork Sausage

Makes 6 servings

8 oz. ground hot pork sausage
2 cups water
1/2 tsp. salt
1/4 tsp. black pepper
1/4 tsp. dry mustard
2 pkgs. frozen black eye peas, 10 oz. size

In a large skillet over medium heat, add the pork sausage. Stir frequently to break the sausage into crumbles as it cooks. Cook about 6-7 minutes or until the sausage is well browned and no longer pink. Drain off the excess grease.

Stir in the water, salt, black pepper, dry mustard and black eye peas. Bring the peas to a boil and place a lid on the skillet. Reduce the heat to low and simmer for 45 minutes or until the peas are tender. Remove the pan from the heat and serve.

My family likes this served with hot biscuits or crusty rolls. We use the biscuits or rolls to sop up any juice.

Hot & Spicy Pepperoni Black Eye Peas

Makes 8 servings

2 cans black eye peas, 15 oz. size
2 oz. sliced pepperoni, diced
1 green bell pepper, diced
1 onion, diced
1/2 tsp. Tabasco sauce
2 tbs. hot taco sauce

In a large sauce pan over low heat, add all the ingredients. Stir until combined. Place a lid on the pan and simmer for 45 minutes. Stir occasionally to keep the peas from sticking. Remove the pan from the heat and serve.

Mexican Black Eye Peas

Makes 10 servings

1 lb. pkg. dried black eye peas
Water
2 lbs. ground pork sausage
1 onion, finely chopped
28 oz. can diced tomatoes, undrained
2 1/2 tbs. finely chopped celery
2 tbs. granulated sugar
2 1/2 tbs. chili powder
2 tsp. garlic salt
1/4 tsp. black pepper

In a large pot, add the black eye peas. Cover the peas with cold water about 3" above the peas. Place a lid on the pot and let the peas soak for 12 hours. Pour the water off the peas and rinse the peas with fresh cold water.

In a skillet over medium heat, add the pork sausage and onion. Stir frequently to break the meat into crumbles as it cooks. Cook about 8-10 minutes or until the sausage is well browned and no longer pink. Drain off the excess grease. Remove the skillet from the heat and add the sausage and onion to the peas.

Stir in the tomatoes, 1 1/2 cups water, celery, granulated sugar, chili powder, garlic salt and black pepper. Bring the peas to a boil. When the peas are boiling, reduce the heat to low. Place a lid on the pot and simmer about 1 1/2 hours or until the peas are tender. Add additional water if needed to keep the peas covered in water while they cook. Remove the pot from the heat and serve.

Hopping Good Peas & Tomatoes

Makes 8 servings

I serve this as a main dish with hot crusty cornbread and chow chow relish.

16 oz. can petite diced tomatoes
4 cups frozen black eye peas
1 ham hock
1 cup chopped onion
1 cup chopped celery
2 tsp. salt
2 tsp. chili powder
1/4 tsp. dried basil
1 bay leaf
1 cup uncooked rice

In a dutch oven over medium heat, add the tomatoes with any juice, black eye peas, ham hock, onion, celery, salt, chili powder, basil and bay leaf. Stir until well combined. Stir frequently and cook for 20 minutes. Add the rice to the pot. Stir until combined. Add water if needed to cover the peas and rice in water. Place a lid on the pot and simmer about 20 minutes or until the rice is tender and the liquid absorbed.

Remove the pot from the heat. Remove the ham hock from the pot. Remove the meat from the ham hock and add the meat back to the pot. Stir until combined and serve.

Savory Black Eye Pea Turnovers

Makes 6 servings

2 cups all purpose flour
1/2 tsp. baking soda
3/4 tsp. salt
1/2 cup vegetable shortening
1 tbs. vinegar
1/4 cup water
1/2 lb. ground beef
1 cup cooked black eye peas
1/4 tsp. garlic powder
1/2 cup shredded American cheese
Vegetable oil for frying

To make the pastry, add the all purpose flour, baking soda, 1/2 teaspoon salt and vegetable shortening to a mixing bowl. Using a pastry cutter, cut the shortening into the dry ingredients until you have coarse crumbs. Stir in the vinegar and water. Only stir until the vinegar and water is incorporated into the dough. Cover the bowl with a damp cloth. Let the dough rest for 20 minutes.

In a skillet over medium heat, add the ground beef. Stir frequently and break the ground beef into crumbles as it cooks. Cook about 6 minutes or until the ground beef is browned and no longer pink. Drain off the excess grease. Stir in the black eye peas, 1/4 teaspoon salt, garlic powder and American cheese. Cook only until the cheese melts and the peas are warm. Remove the pan from the heat.

Roll the dough on a lightly floured surface to about an 1/8" thickness. Cut the dough into six 6" circles. Spoon equal amounts of the beef and pea mixture over one half of each circle. Fold the dough half over the filling. Using your fingers or the tines of a fork, seal the edges of the turnovers. Make sure your edges are well sealed or the filling will leak out when dropped in the hot oil.

In a deep pot, add vegetable oil to a 3" depth in the pot. Heat over medium high heat until the oil reaches 375°. When the oil is ready, carefully add the turnovers. Fry about 3 minutes or until the turnovers are done and golden brown. Remove the turnovers from the oil and drain on paper towels.

Note: For the meatless eaters in my family, I omit the ground beef and use meatless crumbles such as Boca crumbles.

Black Eye Pea Pinwheels

Makes about 6 dozen appetizers

15 oz. can black eye peas, drained
1/4 cup unsalted butter
1/4 tsp. season salt
1/8 tsp. Tabasco sauce
1/8 tsp. garlic powder
6 oz. cream cheese, softened
10 oz. pkg. thinly sliced deli ham
10 green onions, cut into 6" lengths

In a sauce pan over medium heat, add the black eye peas, butter, season salt, Tabasco sauce and garlic powder. Stir constantly and bring the peas to a boil. Reduce the heat to low and simmer for 15 minutes. Stir occasionally after the peas come to a boil. Remove the pan from the heat and cool completely before proceeding to the next step.

When the peas are cool, add the peas and cream cheese to a food processor. Process only until the mixture is well blended. Place about 3 tablespoons of the cream cheese pea mixture on each ham slice. Place a green onion piece in the center of the ham slice. Roll the ham slice up lengthwise. Chill the slices until firm. Cut each ham slice into 1/2" slices and place on a serving platter.

Black Eye Pea Spread

Makes about 3 dozen appetizers

10 oz. pkg. frozen spinach, thawed and all moisture removed
16 oz. can black eye peas, drained
8 oz. can sliced water chestnuts, drained and chopped
1 cup sour cream
1/2 cup dry vegetable soup mix
1/8 tsp. garlic powder
36 slices pumpernickel party bread

In a mixing bowl, add the spinach, black eye peas, water chestnuts, sour cream, dry vegetable soup mix and garlic powder. Stir until well combined. Spread the mixture on the bread slices and serve. You can toast the bread if desired.

South of the Border Black Eye Peas

Makes 8 servings

1 lb. pkg. dried black eye peas
Water
4 oz. smoked ham hock
1 whole jalapeno pepper
2 tbs. dry onion soup mix
2 tsp. chili powder
1 tsp. salt
1/4 tsp. black pepper

Rinse the black eye peas with cold water. Remove any bad peas if needed. Add the peas to a large dutch oven or pot. Cover the peas with cold water about 3" above the peas. Place a lid on the pot and let the peas soak overnight or at least 12 hours.

Drain all the water from the peas. Add 5 cups cold water, ham hock, jalapeno pepper, onion soup mix, chili powder, salt and black pepper to the peas. Stir until combined. Place the pot on the stove over medium heat and bring the peas to a boil. Place a lid on the pot and reduce the heat to low. Simmer for 1 to 1 1/2 hours or until the peas are tender. Remove the pot from the heat. Remove the jalapeno pepper from the peas and discard the pepper. Serve with hot cornbread.

Chunky Black Eye Pea Salsa

Makes 2 cups

1 poblano chile pepper
2 cups cooked black eye peas, rinsed and drained
2/3 cup chopped ripe mango
1/4 cup chopped onion
1/4 cup chopped red bell pepper
1/4 cup chopped fresh cilantro
1/2 tsp. grated lime zest
3 tbs. fresh lime juice
2 tsp. olive oil
1/4 tsp. salt
1/4 tsp. black pepper

Place the poblano pepper on a baking sheet. Turn the oven to the broiler position. Place the pan in the oven and broil the poblano pepper until blistered. Turn the pepper so the pepper blisters on both sides. Remove the pepper from the oven and place the pepper in a Ziploc bag. Let the pepper sit for 10 minutes. Remove the skin from the pepper and discard the seeds. Dice the pepper.

Add the poblano pepper, black eye peas, mango, onion, red bell pepper, cilantro, lime zest, lime juice, olive oil, salt and black pepper to a mixing bowl. Stir until combined. Cover the bowl and refrigerate until well chilled. Serve with tortilla chips if desired. This salsa is also delicious over most meats.

Texas Caviar

Makes about 7 cups

4 cups cooked black eye peas, drained
15 oz. can white hominy, drained
2 tomatoes, chopped
4 green onions, chopped
1 green bell pepper, chopped
1 jalapeno pepper, chopped
1/2 cup chopped onion
1/2 cup chopped fresh parsley
1 cup Italian salad dressing

Add all the ingredients to a large bowl. Toss until well combined. Cover the bowl and refrigerate at least 2 hours before serving. Serve this dish over lettuce for a refreshing salad or with tortilla chips as a dip.

Black Eye Pea Hummus

Makes 1 3/4 cups

3 green onions, sliced
1 garlic clove, peeled
1 jalapeno pepper, halved and seeded
4 sprigs fresh cilantro
15 oz. can black eye peas, rinsed and drained
1/2 cup tahini
3 tbs. lemon juice
1/2 tsp. salt
1/4 tsp. ground cumin
2 tbs. olive oil

In a food processor, add the green onions, garlic, jalapeno pepper and cilantro. Process the mixture until smooth. Scrape down the food processor bowl if needed. Add the black eye peas, tahini, lemon juice, salt and cumin. Puree until smooth.

With the food processor running, slowly add the olive oil. Process until combined. Spoon the hummus into a bowl. Cover the bowl and chill if desired.

Spicy Black Eye Pea Dip

Makes 6 cups

1 3/4 cups dried black eye peas
Water
5 jalapeno peppers, seeded and chopped
1/3 cup chopped onion
1 garlic clove, peeled
1 cup unsalted butter
2 cups shredded sharp American cheese
4 oz. can chopped green chiles
1 tbs. Tabasco sauce

Rinse the black eye peas with cold water. Place the peas in a large sauce pan. Cover the peas with cold water about 2" above the peas. Place the pan over medium heat and bring the peas to a boil. Boil the peas for 2 minutes. Remove the peas from the heat and place a lid on the pan. Let the peas soak for 1 hour.

When the peas have soaked, drain all the water from the peas. Add 5 cups water to the peas and place the peas back on the stove over medium heat. Bring the peas to a boil. Place a lid on the pan and reduce the heat to low. Simmer the peas about 1 1/2 hours or until the peas are tender.

Remove the peas from the heat and drain all the water from the peas. Cool the peas for 15 minutes. Add the peas, jalapeno peppers, onion and garlic to a food processor. Blend until smooth.

In the top of a double boiler over low heat, add the butter and American cheese. Stir constantly and cook until the cheese and butter are melted. Add the green chiles, Tabasco sauce and the black eye pea mixture. Stir until combined and heated. Remove the pan from the heat and spoon into a serving bowl. Serve the dip with corn chips or fresh vegetables.

Chili Black Eye Pea Dip

Makes about 5 cups

16 oz. can black eye peas, drained
16 oz. Velveeta, cubed
10 oz. can chili without beans
4 oz. can diced green chiles
1 large onion, chopped
1 tsp. ground cumin
1 tsp. dried oregano
1/4 tsp. garlic powder
1/2 tsp. Tabasco sauce

Preheat the oven to 350°. Spray an 8" square pan with non stick cooking spray. Add all the ingredients to a food processor. Process until smooth. Spoon the dip into the prepared pan. Bake for 40 minutes. The dip should be hot and bubbly when ready. Remove the dip from the oven and serve.

Black Eye Pea Queso

Makes 3 cups

1/2 cup unsalted butter
1 onion, finely chopped
2 garlic cloves, finely minced
1 lb. Velveeta cheese, cubed
5 jalapeno peppers, chopped
4 cups cooked black eye peas, drained

You can leave the seeds in the jalapeno peppers or remove the seeds depending upon your taste. In a large skillet over medium heat, add the butter, onion and garlic. Saute the onion and garlic for 4 minutes or until the onion is tender.

Add the Velveeta cheese and reduce the heat to low. Stir constantly until the cheese melts. Stir in the jalapeno peppers and the black eye peas. Stir frequently and cook only until the dip is heated. Remove the skillet from the heat and spoon the dip into a serving bowl. Serve with fresh veggies, crackers or chips.

Black Eye Pea and Ham Dip

Makes about 6 cups

1 tsp. vegetable oil
1/2 cup diced cooked country ham
4 cups cooked black eye peas, rinsed and drained
3/4 cup water
1 cup finely diced tomato
2 green onions, sliced
1 celery rib, finely diced
1/4 cup chopped fresh parsley
2 tbs. olive oil
1-2 tbs. apple cider vinegar
Assorted crackers

In a skillet over medium heat, add the vegetable oil and country ham. Saute the ham for 5 minutes. The ham should be well browned. Stir in the black eye peas and 3/4 cup water. Simmer the peas for 7-8 minutes or until most of the liquid evaporates. You will still have some of the liquid in the skillet.

Remove the skillet from the heat. Mash the peas with a fork or potato masher. In a serving bowl, stir together the tomato, green onions, celery, parsley, olive oil and 1 tablespoon apple cider vinegar. Spoon the peas into a serving bowl. Spoon the tomato mixture over the top of the dip. Serve with crackers. You can add the remaining apple cider vinegar if desired. Adjust the vinegar to your taste.

10 LIMA BEANS

In the South, we call them butter beans. Even though different varieties of lima beans abound, we still call all of them butter beans. You can purchase lima beans dried, frozen or canned. If you do not like lima beans, you can substitute most any bean for the lima beans in the recipes.

The most famous dish using lima beans is Succotash. There is a love/hate relationship with most people concerning lima beans. They are delicious cooked over low heat with butter, salt and black pepper. They make a rich broth that is delicious.

Bacon and Beef Succotash

Makes 4 servings

6 slices bacon
3/4 lb. ground chuck
1 onion, chopped
2 cups frozen lima beans
1 cup water
2 cups frozen whole kernel corn
Salt and black pepper to taste

In a skillet over medium heat, add the bacon. Cook the bacon until crisp. Remove the bacon from the skillet and drain on paper towels. Crumble the bacon into bite size pieces. Leave the bacon drippings in the skillet.

Add the ground chuck and onion to the skillet. Stir frequently and break the ground chuck into crumbles as it cooks. Cook for 5-6 minutes or until the ground chuck is browned and no longer pink. Drain the excess grease from the skillet.

Add the lima beans, water and corn to the skillet. Bring the succotash to a boil. Place a lid on the skillet and simmer for 20 minutes. Stir occasionally to keep the beans and corn from sticking to the skillet. Season to taste with salt and black pepper. Remove the skillet from the heat. Spoon the succotash into bowls and sprinkle the bacon over the top of each bowl.

Indian Succotash

Makes 6 servings

1 1/2 cups whole kernel corn, cooked
2 cups lima beans, cooked
2 tbs. unsalted butter
1/2 cup light cream
Salt and black pepper to taste

In a sauce pan over medium low heat, add the corn, lima beans, butter and cream. Stir until well combined and the butter is melted. Simmer for 5 minutes or until the dish is hot and bubbly. Remove the pan from the heat and season with salt and black pepper to taste.

Lima Beans with Canadian Bacon

Makes 6 servings

4 cups fresh lima beans
1 1/4 tsp. salt
6 slices Canadian bacon, chopped
2 tbs. unsalted butter
2 tbs. chopped onion
2 tbs. all purpose flour
2 tsp. light brown sugar
1/4 tsp. ground turmeric
1/8 tsp. black pepper
3 fresh tomatoes, peeled and chopped

In a sauce pan over medium heat, add the lima beans. Cover the beans with water and add 1 teaspoon salt. Bring the lima beans to a boil. Place a lid on the pan and reduce the heat to low. Simmer the lima beans for 20-30 minutes or until the beans are tender. Remove the pan from the heat. Drain the beans but reserve the cooking liquid in a cup.

In a skillet over medium heat, add the Canadian bacon. Stir constantly and brown the bacon about 3 minutes. Remove the bacon from the skillet and set aside. Add the butter to the skillet. When the butter melts, add the onion. Saute the onion for 3 minutes. Stir in the all purpose flour, brown sugar, 1/4 teaspoon salt, turmeric, black pepper, beans and 1 cup bean cooking liquid. If the beans did not have 1 cup liquid, then add water to make one cup. Stir constantly and cook until the dish is thoroughly heated. Remove the skillet from the heat.

Preheat the oven to 350°. Spray a 1 1/2 quart casserole dish with non stick cooking spray. Spoon half of the lima beans into the casserole dish. Place the tomatoes and bacon over the beans. Spoon the remaining lima beans over the tomatoes and bacon. Place aluminum foil over the dish and bake for 20 minutes. Remove the dish from the oven and serve.

Lima Beans & Carrots with Savory Sauce

Makes 6 servings

2 cups fresh lima beans
1 1/2 cups baby carrots
3 tbs. unsalted butter, melted
2 tbs. all purpose flour
1 1/2 cups chicken broth
1 egg yolk, beaten
3 tbs. whipping cream
1 tbs. minced fresh parsley
1/2 tsp. dried savory
1/8 tsp. black pepper

In a sauce pan over medium heat, add the lima beans. Cover the lima beans with water and bring the beans to a boil. Place a lid on the pan and reduce the heat to medium low. Simmer the beans for 20-30 minutes or until the beans are tender. Remove the pan from the heat and drain all the water from the lima beans.

In a sauce pan over medium heat, add the baby carrots. Cover the carrots with water and bring the carrots to a boil. Place a lid on the pan and reduce the heat to medium low. Simmer the carrots about 15 minutes or until they are tender. Remove the pan from the heat and drain all the water from the carrots.

While the vegetables are cooking, make the sauce. In a heavy sauce pan over medium heat, add 2 tablespoons butter and the all purpose flour. Stir constantly and cook for 1 minute. Continue stirring and slowly whisk in the chicken broth.

In a small bowl, whisk together the egg yolk and whipping cream. Slowly whisk in 1/4 cup sauce from the pan. Stir constantly and slowly add the egg mixture to the sauce pan. Stir constantly until the sauce begins to thicken. Stir in the parsley, savory and black pepper. Remove the pan from the heat.

In a 2 quart casserole dish, add the lima beans, carrots and 1 tablespoon butter. Toss until well combined. Pour the sauce over the vegetables. Preheat the oven to 350°. Bake the dish for 25 minutes or until the dish is hot and bubbly.

Old Fashioned Creole Lima Beans

Makes 6 servings

2 slices bacon, diced
2 cups fresh or frozen lima beans, cooked
1/3 cup chopped onion
1/4 cup chopped green bell pepper
1/2 tsp. salt
1/8 tsp. black pepper
16 oz. can diced tomatoes
2 tsp. molasses

In a sauce pan over medium heat, add the bacon. Saute the bacon until crispy. Remove the bacon from the pan and drain on paper towels. Add the lima beans, onion, green bell pepper, salt, black pepper, tomatoes with liquid and molasses. Stir frequently and simmer for 5 minutes. Remove the pan from the heat and pour the beans into a serving bowl. Sprinkle the bacon over the top and serve.

Apple Glazed Lima Beans

Makes 6 servings

2 tbs. unsalted butter
1 onion, sliced
1 apple, cored and sliced
2 cups cooked fresh or frozen lima beans
3 tbs. light brown sugar

In a sauce pan over medium heat, add the butter, onion and apple. Stir frequently and saute until the onion and apple are tender. On my stove, it takes about 5 minutes. Stir in the lima beans and brown sugar. Saute for 5 minutes or until the brown sugar is melted and the lima beans are warm. Remove the pan from the heat and serve.

Lima Bean Garden Casserole

Makes 6 servings

2 cups fresh lima beans
1 teaspoon salt
1 cup fresh corn, cut from the cob
2 tbs. unsalted butter
2 tbs. all purpose flour
1 cup whole milk
1/4 tsp. dried dill
1/8 tsp. black pepper
1 cup shredded carrots
1/4 cup grated Parmesan cheese

In a sauce pan over medium heat, add the lima beans and 1/2 teaspoon salt. Cover the beans with water and bring the beans to a boil. When the beans are at a full boil, place a lid on the pan. Reduce the heat to low and simmer the beans about 20 minutes. Add the fresh corn to the beans and cook about 10-15 minutes or until the beans and corn are tender. Remove the pan from the heat and drain all the water from the pan.

In a heavy sauce pan over medium heat, add the butter. When the butter melts, stir in the all purpose flour. Stir constantly and cook for 2 minutes. Slowly add the milk to the pan. Stir constantly and cook until the sauce thickens and bubbles. Stir in the dill, 1/2 teaspoon salt, black pepper and carrots. Remove the pan from the heat.

Preheat the oven to 350°. Spray a 2 quart casserole dish with non stick cooking spray. Add the beans and corn to the dish along with the sauce. Stir until well combined. Bake for 25 minutes. Sprinkle the Parmesan cheese over the top of the dish. Bake for 5-10 minutes or until the cheese is melted and lightly browned. Remove the casserole from the oven and serve.

Savory Lima Beans

Makes 4 servings

2 cups fresh lima beans
3/4 tsp. salt
2 slices bacon
1/2 cup water
1 tbs. all purpose flour
2 tbs. chopped onion
1 tbs. light brown sugar
1/4 tsp. celery salt
1/4 tsp. paprika

In a sauce pan over medium heat, add the lima beans and 1/2 teaspoon salt. Cover the beans with water and bring to a boil. When the beans are at a full boil, place a lid on the pan. Reduce the heat to low and simmer the beans about 25 minutes or until the beans are tender. Remove the pan from the heat and drain all the water from the pan.

In a skillet over medium heat, add the bacon. Cook the bacon about 7 minutes or until the bacon is almost crisp. Remove the bacon from the skillet and drain on paper towels. Preheat the oven to 375°. Spray a 1 quart baking dish with non stick cooking spray. In a small bowl, whisk together the water and all purpose flour. Add the flour and water, lima beans, onion, brown sugar, 1/4 teaspoon salt, celery salt and paprika to the casserole dish. Stir until well combined. Lay the bacon slices over the top. Bake for 20 minutes or until the beans thicken and the bacon is crispy. Remove the dish from the oven and serve.

Swiss Lima Bean Casserole

Makes 8 servings

4 cups fresh lima beans
Salt and black pepper to season
1/4 cup unsalted butter
3 tbs. all purpose flour
2 1/2 cups whole milk
2 cups shredded Swiss cheese
4 oz. can sliced mushrooms, drained
3 tbs. grated onion
1/2 cup sliced almonds, toasted

In a sauce pan over medium heat, add the lima beans and 1 teaspoon salt. Cover the beans with water and bring the beans to a boil. Reduce the heat to medium low and place a lid on the pan. Simmer the beans for 20-30 minutes or until the beans are tender. Remove the pan from the heat and drain all the water from the beans.

In a sauce pan over medium heat, add the butter. When the butter melts, stir in the all purpose flour. Stir constantly and cook for 1 minute. Keep stirring and add the whole milk. Cook until the sauce thickens and bubbles. Add the Swiss cheese and stir until the cheese melts. Remove the pan from the heat.

Preheat the oven to 350°. Pour the beans, sauce, mushrooms, onion and almonds in a 2 quart casserole dish. Stir until well combined. Season to taste with salt and black pepper if desired. Bake for 20 minutes or until the beans are hot and bubbly. Remove the dish from the oven and serve.

Lima Beans Deluxe

Makes 6 servings

2 tbs. unsalted butter
2 tbs. all purpose flour
1 cup whole milk
1 tsp. salt
1/4 tsp. black pepper
2 cups cooked lima beans
1/2 cup chopped red pimento
1 cup shredded cheddar cheese
2 tbs. ketchup
2 tbs. melted unsalted butter
1/2 cup soft breadcrumbs

In a skillet over medium heat, add 2 tablespoons unsalted butter. When the butter melts and sizzles, stir in the all purpose flour. Stir constantly and cook for 1 minute. Keep stirring and add the whole milk, salt and black pepper. Cook until the sauce thickens and bubbles.

Preheat the oven to 375°. Spray a 2 quart casserole dish with non stick cooking spray. Stir the lima beans, red pimento, cheddar cheese and ketchup into the sauce. Remove the pan from the heat and pour the mixture into the casserole dish.

In a small bowl, toss the breadcrumbs with 2 tablespoons melted unsalted butter. Sprinkle the breadcrumbs over the top of the casserole. Bake for 30 minutes or until the dish is hot, bubbly and the top golden brown. Remove the dish from the oven and serve.

Lima Bean Cheese Casserole

Makes 6 servings

4 slices bacon
1/2 cup chopped onion
10.75 oz. can condensed cheddar cheese soup
1/2 cup sour cream
4 cups cooked lima beans
1/4 cup dry breadcrumbs
1 tbs. unsalted butter, melted

In a skillet over medium heat, add the bacon. Cook the bacon about 5 minutes or until the bacon is crisp. Remove the bacon from the pan and drain on paper towels.

Add the onion to the bacon drippings in the pan. Saute about 5 minutes or until the onion is tender. Stir in the cheddar cheese soup and sour cream. Stir constantly and cook only until the soup is thoroughly heated. Remove the pan from the heat and stir in the lima beans and bacon.

Spray a 2 quart casserole dish with non stick cooking spray. Preheat the oven to 375°. Spoon the lima beans into the casserole dish. Sprinkle the dry breadcrumbs over the top. Drizzle the melted butter over the breadcrumbs. Bake for 20 minutes or until the casserole is hot and bubbly. Remove the dish from the oven and serve.

Beef & Lima Bean Dinner

Makes 4 servings

1 lb. ground beef
1 onion, chopped
16 oz. can lima beans with liquid
3/4 cup barbecue sauce
1 cup shredded cheddar cheese
5 oz. can refrigerated biscuits (5 biscuits per can)

In a skillet over medium heat, add the ground beef and onion. Stir frequently to break the meat into crumbles as it cooks. Cook about 7 minutes or until the ground beef is well browned and no longer pink. Remove the skillet from the heat and drain off the excess grease. Stir in the lima beans and barbecue sauce.

Preheat the oven to 375°. Spray a 2 quart casserole dish with non stick cooking spray. Spoon the ground beef and beans into the casserole dish. Sprinkle the cheddar cheese over the top. Cut each biscuit in half. Place the biscuit pieces over the cheese. Bake for 25 minutes or until the biscuits are golden brown. Remove the casserole from the oven and serve.

You can substitute any can of beans for the lima beans if desired.

Chili Lima Bean Pot

Makes 6 servings

2 cups fresh lima beans
1/2 lb. ground beef
2 onions, sliced
1 garlic clove, minced
28 oz. can diced tomatoes, drained
1 tsp. crushed red pepper flakes
1 tsp. salt
1 tsp. chili powder
1/2 cup shredded cheddar cheese

In a sauce pan over medium heat, add the lima beans. Cover the beans with water. Simmer the beans for 25 minutes. The beans will not be done at this point but should be almost tender. Remove the pan from the heat. Drain the lima beans but reserve 1 cup bean liquid.

In a large sauce pan over medium heat, add the ground beef, onions and garlic. Stir frequently to break the ground beef into crumbles as it cooks. Cook about 6 minutes or until the ground beef is well browned and no longer pink. Drain off the excess grease. Stir in the lima beans and 1 cup bean liquid. Stir in the tomatoes, red pepper flakes, salt and chili powder. Bring the beans and beef to a boil. Reduce the heat to low and place a lid on the pan. Simmer for 45 minutes. Add the cheddar cheese and stir until combined. Simmer for 10 minutes. Remove the pan from the heat and serve.

Two Bean Pork Succotash

Makes 6 servings

4 ears yellow corn, husked and silk removed
8 oz. fresh green beans or about 3 cups
1/4 lb. salt pork, cubed
2 cups fresh lima beans
1/2 cup light cream
Salt and black pepper to taste

Remove the corn from the cob and set aside. Cut the green beans into 1" pieces. Trim the ends from the green beans. In a skillet over medium low heat, add the salt pork. Stir frequently and cook the salt pork until browned, crispy and done. Remove the skillet from the heat. Drain the salt pork on paper towels.

In a sauce pan over medium heat, add the green beans and lima beans. Cover the beans with water. Add a pinch of salt to the beans. Simmer for 15-20 minutes or until the beans are tender. Add the corn and simmer for 5-10 minutes or until the corn is tender.

Drain most of the water from the beans. Stir in the light cream and season to taste with salt and black pepper. Remove the pan from the heat and pour into a bowl. Sprinkle the salt pork over the top and serve. You can use frozen green beans, lima beans and corn if desired.

Butter Beans with Pecans

Makes 4 servings

1 beef bouillon cube
1/2 cup hot water
2 cups cooked butter beans
1/2 cup chopped pecans
1 cup onion, chopped
1/8 tsp. Worcestershire sauce
1/2 cup shredded American cheese
1/3 cup soft bread crumbs
2 tbs. unsalted butter

Preheat the oven to 350°. In a small bowl, add the beef bouillon cube and water. Stir until the bouillon cube is dissolved. In a 2 quart casserole dish, add the butter beans, beef bouillon, pecans, onion, Worcestershire sauce and American cheese. Stir until combined.

Sprinkle the bread crumbs over the top of the casserole. Cut the butter into pieces and place over the bread crumbs. Bake for 30 minutes or until the dish is bubbly and the top lightly toasted. Remove the dish from the oven and serve.

Lima Bacon Bake

Makes 6 servings

2 pkgs. frozen lima beans, 10 oz. size
1 1/2 cups water
6 slices bacon, diced
1 cup chopped onion
1/2 cup chopped celery
1 cup shredded Monterey Jack cheese
1/4 tsp. Worcestershire sauce
1/4 tsp. black pepper

In a sauce pan over medium heat, add the lima beans and water. Bring the beans to a boil. Place a lid on the pan and reduce the heat to low. Simmer the lima beans about 15-20 minutes or until the lima beans are tender. Remove the pan from the heat. Drain the water from the beans but keep 1/2 cup bean liquid to use later in the recipe.

In a large skillet over medium heat, add the bacon. Cook the bacon only until done but still pliable. The bacon will cook further in the oven. Remove the bacon from the skillet and drain on paper towels. Leave the bacon drippings in the skillet. Add the onion and celery to the skillet. Saute the vegetables about 5 minutes. Stir in the lima beans, Monterey Jack cheese, Worcestershire sauce and black pepper. Remove the pan from the heat.

Preheat the oven to 350°. Spray a 2 quart casserole dish with non stick cooking spray. Spoon the bean mixture into the casserole dish. Sprinkle the bacon over the top of the dish. Bake for 25 minutes or until the dish is hot, bubbly and the bacon crispy. Remove the dish from the oven and serve.

Baked Lima Bean & Pear Casserole

Makes 6 servings

1 lb. dried lima beans
6 cups water
Salt and black pepper to taste
29 oz. can pear halves
1/2 cup melted unsalted butter
1 cup light brown sugar

Add the lima beans and water to a stock pot. Place the pot on the stove over medium heat and bring the beans to a boil. Boil for 3 minutes. Remove the beans from the heat and place a lid on the pot. Let the beans soak for 1 hour.

Place the beans back on the stove over medium heat. Bring the beans to a boil and simmer for 1 1/2 -2 hours or until the beans are tender. Add additional water if needed to keep the beans covered with water while cooking.

Remove the beans from the heat and drain all the water from the beans. Season the beans to taste with salt and black pepper. Drain the pears but reserve 1/2 cup pear juice. In a small bowl, stir together the melted butter, pear juice and brown sugar. Dice the pears into cubes.

Preheat the oven to 325°. In a large shallow casserole dish, add half of the beans. Pour half of the butter brown sugar mixture over the beans. Place half of the pears over the beans. Repeat the layering process one more time using the remaining beans, brown sugar mixture and pears. Cover the dish with aluminum foil. Bake for 2 hours. Remove the dish from the oven and serve.

Fresh Lima Bean Casserole

Makes 4 servings

2 cups fresh lima beans
1/2 cup chopped onion
1/2 cup chopped green bell pepper
1/4 cup melted unsalted butter
10.75 oz can cream of celery soup
1/2 cup shredded cheddar cheese
1/2 cup butter cracker crumbs

In a sauce pan over medium heat, add the lima beans. Cover the beans with water and bring the beans to a boil. Simmer the beans for 15 minutes or until the beans are tender. Remove the beans from the heat and drain all the water from the beans.

Preheat the oven to 350°. Spray a 1 quart casserole dish with non stick cooking spray. In a skillet over medium heat, add the onion, green bell pepper and butter. Saute the onion and green bell pepper for 4 minutes. Remove the skillet from the heat.

Add the lima beans, onion and green bell pepper with butter and cream of celery soup to the casserole dish. Stir until well combined. Bake for 25 minutes or until the dish is hot and bubbly. Sprinkle the cheddar cheese and butter cracker crumbs over the top of the beans. Bake for 5 minutes or until the cheese is melted and the crackers golden brown. Remove the dish from the oven and serve.

Marinated Lima Beans

Makes 6 servings

3 cups fresh lima beans
2 tbs. chopped green bell pepper
2 tbs. chopped green onion
1/3 cup vinegar
1/4 cup granulated sugar
1/4 cup vegetable oil
1 tbs. prepared horseradish

In a sauce pan over medium heat, add the lima beans. Cover the beans with water and bring the beans to a boil. Simmer the beans for 25 minutes or until the beans are tender. Remove the beans from the heat and drain all the water from the beans. Rinse the beans with cold water and drain all the water again.

Place the beans in a mixing bowl. Add the green bell pepper and green onion. In a glass jar with a lid, add the vinegar, granulated sugar, vegetable oil and horseradish. Place the lid on the jar and shake until well combined. Pour the dressing over the beans. Toss until well combined. Cover the bowl and refrigerate for 4 hours before serving. Toss the salad again before serving.

Spanish Cheese Lima Beans

Makes 6 servings

2 1/2 cups fresh lima beans
1 cup thinly sliced celery
1/2 cup finely chopped onion
2 tbs. vegetable oil
3 tomatoes, peeled and chopped
2 tsp. Worcestershire sauce
1/2 tsp. salt
1/8 tsp. black pepper
Dash of Tabasco sauce
1 1/2 cups shredded American cheese

In a sauce pan over medium heat, add the lima beans. Cover the beans with water and bring the beans to a boil. Simmer the beans for 25 minutes or until the beans are tender. Remove the beans from the heat and drain all the water from the beans.

In a skillet over medium heat, add the celery, onion and vegetable oil. Saute the vegetables for 4 minutes. Add the tomatoes and stir until combined. Reduce the heat to low and place a lid on the skillet. Simmer the tomatoes for 10 minutes. Stir frequently to keep the tomatoes from burning and sticking.

Add the lima beans, Worcestershire sauce, salt, black pepper and Tabasco sauce to the skillet. Stir frequently and simmer for 10 minutes. Remove the skillet from the heat. Preheat the oven to 350°. Spray a 2 quart casserole dish with non stick cooking spray.

Spoon half of the bean mixture into the casserole dish. Sprinkle 3/4 cup American cheese over the beans. Spoon the remaining bean mixture over the cheese. Bake for 20 minutes. Sprinkle 3/4 cup American cheese over the top of the dish. Bake for 5 minutes or until the cheese is melted and bubbly. Remove the dish from the oven and serve.

Chapter Index

Bean Soups & Stews

White Bean Chowder with Sage Pesto, 2
Spicy Chicken Bean Chili, 3
Vegetarian Chili, 4
Vegetarian Pinto Bean Chili, 5
Cow Puncher's Bean Stew, 6
Guadalajara Soup, 7
Simple Mexican Puchero, 8
Spicy Three Bean Soup, 9
Mexican Black Bean Soup, 10
One Skillet Chili Bake, 11
Bean and Pasta Soup, 12
Carolina Black Bean Soup, 13
Cabbage Bean Soup, 16
Spanish Chickpea Soup, 14
Western Bean Stew, 15
Baked Bean Winter Soup, 16
Senate Bean Soup, 17
Sausage, Spinach and Bean Soup, 18
Refried Bean Soup, 19
Tuscany Bean Soup, 20
White Bean Soup, 21
Portuguese Bean Soup, 22
Kidney Bean Soup with Walnuts, 23
Bean and Hominy Soup, 24
White Bean & Collard Green Soup, 25
Navy Bean Squash Soup, 26
Black, White & Red Soup, 27
Spicy White Bean Soup, 27
Beanolla Soup, 28
Lentil Vegetable Soup, 29
Sausage Lentil Soup, 30
Navy Bean Soup with Ham Hocks, 31
Ham and Bean Soup, 32
Creamy Lentil Soup, 33
Ham Lentil Soup, 34
Spinach Bean Soup, 35

Country Pea Soup, 36
Hearty Bean and Barley Soup, 37
White Bean Pot, 38
Bean Counter Soup, 39
Ham and Black Eye Pea Stew, 40

Pinto Beans

Navajo Tacos with Turkey Pinto Bean Topping, 42
Skillet Veggie & Bean Tacos, 43
Chicken and Bean Tacos, 44
Spicy Bean Enchiladas, 45
Three Bean Enchiladas, 46
Ranch Chili & Beans, 47
Southwestern Beans, 48
Spicy Hot Beans, 49
Mexican Pinto Beans, 50
Pinto Beans with Spareribs, 51
Hearty Pinto Beans with Sausage, 52
Easy Bean and Cheese Chimichangas, 53
Razorback Beans, 54
Ranch House Beans, 53
Pinto Bean Chalupas, 55
Bean Burrito Appetizers, 56
Easy Cheesy Smoked Sausage with Beans Casserole, 57
Sweet Hot Pinto Beans, 58
Frijoles Rancheros, 59
Pinto Bean Enchilada Stack, 60
Picante Bean Sauce, 61
Chili Bean Dip, 61
Prairie Fire Bean Dip, 62
Pinto Bean Pie, 62

Kidney Beans

Bean & Mushroom Burritos, 64
Baked Bean Medley, 65
Hot Bean Dish, 66
Vegetarian Saute', 67
Kidney Bean Casserole, 68
Caribbean Beans & Rice, 69
Creole Beans and Rice, 70
Sweet Sour Red Beans, 71
Red Beans and Rice, 72
Smoked Sausage Red Beans & Rice, 73
Slow Cooker Orleans Beans & Rice, 74
Red Beans & Couscous, 75
Spinach Bean Lasagna, 76
Texas Sausage, Beans & Rice, 77
Bean and Cornbread Casserole, 78
Spicy Mexican Bean Casserole, 79
Kidney Bean Salsa, 80
Ham Bone Red Beans & Rice, 81

Lentils

Lentil Burritos, 83
Tomato Baked Lentils, 84
Cheesy Pasta and Lentils, 85
Lentil Tacos, 86
Lentil Samosas, 87
Lentil Burgers, 88
Lentil and Rice Supper, 89
Lentil Rice Casserole, 90
Tex Mex Lentils, 91
Baked Lentils with Cheese, 92
Bean Pot Lentils, 93
Lentil Pate, 94
Lentil Spread, 95

Black Beans

Black Bean & Rice Tostados, 97
Meatless Enchiladas, 98
Spicy Beef and Black Beans, 99
Marinated Black Beans, 99
Meatless Black Bean Casserole, 100
Tomato Bean Sauce Pasta Dinner, 101
Black Bean & Lime Pasta, 102
Black Beans with Rice, 103
Black Bean Pancakes with Gazpacho Butter, 104
Black Bean Cakes with Mixed Greens, 106
Corn Black Bean Cakes with Salmon Salsa, 108
Black Bean Spaghetti, 107
Cuban Black Beans, 109
Spanish Black Beans, 110
Casserole of Black Beans, 111
Black Bean Chili Marsala, 112
Easy Black Beans with Yellow Rice, 114
Bean Cassoulet with Cornmeal Dumplings, 113
Vegetarian Burritos, 115
Black Bean Pizza Sauce, 116
Black Bean Corn Salsa, 116
Black Bean Guacamole, 117
Black Bean Dip, 117

Great Northern & Navy Beans

Old Fash. Baked Beans with Ham, 119
Zesty Pork & Beans, 120
Can Can Baked Beans, 121
Slow Cooker Bourbon Beans, 121
Baked Pork & Beans with Ham, 122
Molasses Baked Beans, 123
Southern Beef Baked Beans, 124
Hawaiian Baked Beans & Franks, 124
Three Meat Baked Beans, 125
Stove Top Franks N Beans, 126
Fruited Pork & Beans, 126
Beefy Baked Beans, 127
Old Fash. Boston Baked Beans, 128
Lamb and White Bean Casserole, 129
Turnip Green White Bean Bake, 130
White Beans & Spinach, 131
Rosemary Cannellini Beans, 131
White Bean Hummus, 132
White Bean Spread, 133
White Bean Dip, 134
White Bean Relish, 135

Garbanzo Beans

Chickpea Chipotle Tostadas, 137
Vegetarian Cassoulet, 138
Beef and Garbanzo Bean Dinner, 139
Red Pepper Hummus Pizza, 140
Creamy Dried Tomato Hummus, 141
Quick Hummus, 141
Garbanzo Bean Dip, 140
Herbed Garbanzo Bean Spread, 142
Spaghetti with Garbanzo Bean Sauce, 143

Salads

Bean Salad Sandwiches, 145
Caribbean Shrimp Black Bean Salad, 146
White Bean Tuna Salad, 147
Mexican Chick Pea Salad, 145
Bean and Sausage Salad, 148
Easy Marinated Pasta Bean Salad, 149
Hoppin' John Salad, 150
Hominy Bean Salad, 151
Spicy Bean Salad, 149
Three Pea Salad, 152
Chick Pea Salad, 152
Mediterranean Lentil Salad, 153
Black Bean and Cheese Salad, 154
Kidney Bean Coleslaw, 154
Bean Salad Vinaigrette, 155
Sweet & Sour Bean Salad, 156
Avocado Garbanzo Salad, 155
Full O' Beans Salad, 157
Pasta Bean Salad, 158
Four Bean Salad, 159
Black Bean Salad, 160
Black Bean and Rice Salad, 161
Black Bean and Barley Salad, 162
Kidney Bean Wild Rice Salad, 163
Quick Bean Salad, 163
Chickpea and Fennel Salad, 164
Pinto Bean Salad, 165
Black Eye Pea Salad, 166
Mexican Black Eye Pea Salad, 167
Goat Cheese & Black Eye Pea Salad, 168
Curry Black Eye Pea Salad, 169
Black Eye Pea Vinaigrette Salad, 170
Black Eye Pea Sweet Potato Salad, 171
Bean Relish, 172

Black Eye Peas

Zesty Black Eye Pea Relish, 174
Pickled Black Eye Peas, 174
Plain Ole Black Eye Peas, 175
Chinese Black Eye Peas, 176
Cajun Peas, 177
Black Eye Pea Cakes, 178
Black Eye Pea Spaghetti, 179
Baked Sweet & Sour Peas, 177
Mexican Black Eye Pea Casserole, 180
Marinated Black Eye Peas, 181
Black Eye Pea Skillet Dinner, 181
Black Eye Peas & Ham Hocks, 182
Special Black Eye Peas, 183
Creole Black Eye Peas, 184
Black Eye Pea & Spinach Potatoes, 185
Spicy Black Eye Peas, 186
Old Fashioned Hopping John, 187
Black Eye Peas with Pork Sausage, 188
Hot & Spicy Pepperoni Black Eye Peas, 188
Mexican Black Eye Peas, 189
Hopping Good Peas & Tomatoes, 190
Savory Black Eye Pea Turnovers, 191
Black Eye Pea Pinwheels, 192
Black Eye Pea Spread, 192
South of the Border Black Eye Peas, 193
Chunky Black Eye Pea Salsa, 194
Texas Caviar, 195
Spicy Black Eye Pea Dip, 196
Black Eye Pea Hummus, 195
Chili and Black Eye Pea Dip, 197
Black Eye Pea and Ham Dip, 198
Black Eye Pea Queso, 197

Lima Beans

Bacon and Beef Succotash, 200
Indian Succotash, 200
Lima Beans with Canadian Bacon, 201
Lima Beans & Carrots with Savory Sauce, 202
Old Fashioned Creole Lima Beans, 203
Lima Bean Garden Casserole, 204
Savory Lima Beans, 205
Swiss Lima Bean Casserole, 206
Apple Glazed Lima Beans, 203
Lima Beans Deluxe, 207
Lima Bean Cheese Casserole, 208
Beef & Lima Bean Dinner, 209
Chili Lima Bean Pot, 210
Two Bean Pork Succotash, 211
Butter Beans with Pecans, 212
Lima Bacon Bake, 213
Baked Lima Bean & Pear Casserole, 214
Fresh Lima Bean Casserole, 215
Marinated Lima Beans, 216
Spanish Cheese Lima Beans, 217

ABOUT THE AUTHOR

Lifelong southerner who lives in Bowling Green, KY. Priorities in life are God, family and pets. I love to cook, garden and feed most any stray animal that walks into my yard. I love old cookbooks and cookie jars. Huge NBA fan who loves to spend hours watching basketball games. Enjoy cooking for family and friends and hosting get togethers. Can't wait each year to build gingerbread houses for the kids.

Made in United States
North Haven, CT
26 July 2023